MASTER YOUR MINDSET

A GUIDE TO WIN THE INNER-GAME AND UNLOCK THE POWER OF FLOW

COLLIN HENDERSON

FOREWORD BY CHARLY MARTIN IV

@COLLINHENDERSON

COLLIN HENDERSON

WWW.THECOLLINHENDERSON.COM

PRAISE FOR *MASTER YOUR MINDSET*

Working with Collin to master my mindset has been amazing. I recommend this book to anyone looking to take their mentality to the next level. - *Steven Souza, Jr., Arizona Diamondbacks, MLB*

Mental skills training is a big component of what we emphasize in our program and *Master Your Mindset* is a fantastic resource for coaches to help their athletes win the inner-game. - *Lisa Johnson, Head Coach, University of Idaho Women's Golf*

Whether in sports, business, or other walks of life, the more you can access flow, the better you will perform. This book will help you get there. - *Jason Johnson, Canadian Football League Grey Cup Champion, Founder of Jason Ryan Creative*

Collin's work with our team was vital to our success. I wish I had the tools in this book when I played in high school and college. - *Kali Gesser, Head Women's Volleyball Coach, Pullman High School*

I loved Collin's first book *Project Rise*, but *Master Your Mindset* digs even deeper into the mental skills needed to maximize one's potential as an individual and team. - *Travis Jewett, Head Coach University of Tulane Baseball*

In athletics, the emphasis is usually on being bigger, stronger, and faster. However, sustained success is found from the space in-between the ears—which Collin masterfully lays out for the reader. - *Dave Johnson, Washington State High School Coaches Hall of Fame, Co-Founder of TBI Baseball Camp*

ALL THE WORLD'S A STAGE,

AND ALL THE MEN AND WOMEN

MERELY PLAYERS...

- JAQUES
FROM WILLIAM SHAKESPEARE'S *AS YOU LIKE IT*

FOREWORD

My line on the stat sheet read fourteen catches, 323 yards, and five touchdowns—the best game of my life, and my last college game.

Then...reality hit. We lost 93-68 (that is not a typo...that was really the score), and my football career, for the time being, was over. There were no more guarantees.

As I read *Master Your Mindset* for the first time, I could not help but think about this game and how my mindset was different. How I was in a FLOW state. While I did not have this book ten years ago, there was no doubt Collin's mindset tools and principles were present.

The date was November 22, 2008, a day I will truly never forget. I was in my sixth and final year (yes, sixth) at West Texas A&M University (WTAMU). We were in Abilene, Texas to face second ranked Abilene Christian University (ACU) in the second round of the NCAA Division II playoffs. We came into the game with only one loss, which came one month earlier to ACU at home. They had finished their season with a perfect record, and the rematch was set.

Entering this final college game, I had done all I could and set the stage for the opportunity to make the transition to the next level—my dream of reaching the NFL. There was nothing else I could have done, and I needed it all to put myself in this position. I also knew that getting to the NFL was not going to be easy, and nothing was guaranteed. So yes, this could be it. This could be my last game. I may never wear a jersey again.

There is one thing about football that is just different than other sports. Not better, not worse, just different. You can't play in pick-up leagues at your local health club, and you can't play until you are in your latter stages of life. It just can't happen. Because of these realities, this day felt different than I had ever experienced.

I want to take you to the fourth quarter and the final play from scrimmage. We were on offense with the ball on our own forty-eight-yard line trailing 61-93 with under ten seconds remaining in the game. Clearly, the game was over, but I was not done. I had always told myself I would remember my last play, that final play. The emotions were real and raw. The tears were already building, and no matter how hard I tried, I could not hold them back.

My quarterback and close friend, Keith Null, called the play: very simple, Z–Missile. He called my number...one more chance to make a play...one more chance to do what I loved! I can remember it like it was yesterday. I felt like I was floating. I was locked in, and there was going to be nothing that was going to stop me. I would not allow myself to be tackled until I reached the end zone. I am serious. Those were the thoughts...it was different. You might wonder why it matters since there was no way we could win. My mindset told me otherwise. I was in FLOW...no judgment and filled with a relentless energy. Seven broken tackles and fifty-two yards later, I ended up in the end zone. With no more time on the clock, and after running over the final defender, I was lying in the end zone. I was a mess. I literally took on the whole team and prevailed. Overcome with emotions that had been building for the past twenty-four years, I let it all out and cried like I never cried before.

Fourteen catches, 323 yards, and five touchdowns...that was my game stat-line. What I did not know at the time was that final catch broke the WTAMU and Lone Star Conference record for receiving yards in a single game. It also marked a school and Lone Star Conference record for touchdowns in a single game, along with numerous other records across the school, conference, and NCAA ranks.

One's mental game is what will take you to the next level. It is what will allow you to achieve the success you have been dreaming of. It is what allowed me to achieve my dream. I was blessed to see another day and another jersey. I was fortunate enough to play the game I love for five-and-a-half years in the National Football League. In my years competing at the collegiate and professional levels, mindset is what separates the good from the great.

I am a true believer, and it is very simple: It was beyond the athletic gifts and skills that I possessed. It was a mindset. It was a belief. It was truly understanding the power of the mind and allowing it to lead, guide, and drive my life.

While I may not have realized I was in FLOW back on that November day in 2008, there is no doubt I was, which is why, ten years later, I find myself with this amazing opportunity to write the foreword for this incredible book, written by a role model, mentor, and friend I've always leaned on for advice. The tools that Collin provides in *Master Your Mindset* can be life-changing.

Believe in yourself and in your dreams.

Now GO! And Master Your Mindset!

I love you Collin, and I thank you!

Charly Martin
Five-year NFL veteran
All-American, Hall of Fame,
West Texas A&M University

CONTENTS

INTRODUCTION

It was my first Apple Cup in Pullman, Washington as a football player at Washington State University. We were playing our arch rivals, the University of Washington Huskies. They were having a great year and were one win away from clinching a trip to the Rose Bowl and a Pac-10 (now Pac-12) title. Though we just beat University of Southern California in the Coliseum the week before, we were out of bowl contention with just four wins on the year. Our team and the entire Cougar Nation still had hope though. We could salvage our season by playing the spoiler and upsetting our cross-state rival. We were playing for pride, while the UW Huskies were playing for Pasadena.

These Apple Cup games were always filled with emotion for me because, though I was a devoted Coug, I had many friends, and former fellow Puyallup High School graduates who donned the purple and gold for U-Dub. My high school (whose colors are also purple and gold) was a breeding ground for Husky football. My best friend since fourth grade, Todd Elstrom, was even their best receiver that year. Todd and I grew up cheering for both sides, and would often dream of competing in an Apple Cup. Now, I was actually living that dream.

It was a blistering cold late-November night on the Palouse (a name given to the area around the town of Pullman). Both sidelines were equipped with heated benches, hand warmers, and hot chocolate to help keep the players thawed against the projected thirteen-degree weather. Getting ready, I definitely dressed accordingly in the locker room: Tights...check. Long sleeve thermal...check. Head warmer...check. Heat packets and gloves...check. I was ready for battle.

I left the locker room and jogged under the tunnel with the other specialists: kickers, punters, and returners (I was a wide receiver and punt returner). I could already hear the hyped-up crowd cheering to music getting ready for the big game. While making our way onto the field for pre-game warm-ups, we noticed something strange. As the home team, we always warmed up on the east half of Martin Stadium. But for some reason, the Husky Marching Band had surrounded our half of the field.

What the heck are they doing? I remember thinking.

Maybe they didn't know who warmed up on which side of the field. Maybe they were playing some kind of prank? Or maybe they were attempting to stay close to the away section in the east end zone along with the faithful Husky fans who trekked across the state to hopefully watch history. Either way, the enemy had completely surrounded both of our sidelines and end zone.

To make matters worse, these trespassers were playing "Bow Down to Washington" over and over. To a Husky fan, this battle cry is a sweet symphony of gridiron grit. To the Coug faithful, this intrepid noise is like hearing fingernails running down a chalkboard.

Most of us players thought the band would eventually move to their side of the field, but nothing happened. They just kept playing "Bow Down to Washington" over and over.

"Are they really doing this? And where is our band?" I asked my wide receiver teammate and fellow return specialist, Curtis Nettles.

14

"I don't know," he replied while shaking his head. "This is crazy."

I envisioned the Cougar Marching Band coming to our rescue and protecting our turf like Michael Jackson's music video "Beat It," or a scene from *West Side Story*. I guess college marching bands don't roll like that.

Just think about how bold of a move this is. In my three decades of being either a player or a fan of football, I had never once seen this happen before that game nor have I seen it since. Have you ever witnessed a marching band go onto someone else's field, surround their opponent's team, and play their own fight song over and over? The answer is probably never. This prank was unprecedented.

At that moment, we realized we had to take matters into our own hands. No more waiting for someone outside our team to do something. Somebody in our squad needed to intervene and protect our house. We needed someone to step up. We needed a plan. And in that moment where pride, ego, and bragging rights were at stake, a leader emerged.

Enter to the scene six-foot-five, 225-pound senior quarterback, Paul Menke. Paul knew the significance of this game. This graduate of Lewis and Clark High School grew up in nearby Spokane. Paul was a baller who had played both quarterback and receiver during his Cougar career. He even played a year of basketball for the Cougs and was a fan-favorite at Beasley Coliseum coming off the bench.

Paul was playing his last game of his college football career. He wouldn't let this happen, not on his watch. Paul was known as a phenomenal dual-threat athlete, but he was also known as quite the character. He was very confident, outspoken, and was probably one of the most popular players on the team. If anybody was going to take action, it was

15

Paul.

During wide receiver and quarterback drills, Paul had an idea about how to get the Husky Marching Band off of our side of the field. Over the booming warm-up music, Paul yelled at me, "Collin, Collin! Come here," while waving his hand to come meet him in the middle of the field with the other quarterbacks. Being a respectful underclassman, I jogged over to hear what he wanted.

When I got there he said, "OK, this is what we're gonna do: We're gonna stop this BS and get these guys off our side of the field."

He then added, "OK, C-Hen [my nickname], line up there on the left side and run a ten-yard out route. I'll do the rest."

Many times in sports, there is an unspoken chemistry and understanding between two players. I knew what he was thinking, and we were on the same page.

"OK, Paul. I got you," I said.

I ran over to my position, got into my stance, and ran a crisp ten-yard out route to our sideline. Paul proceeded to throw a tight spiraled pass in my direction, but five yards out of bounds.

The ball, which was clearly out of my grasp, forced a Husky tuba player to move out of the way, and trip onto one of his band mates. This mishap created a domino effect knocking three or four Husky band members down to the frozen tundra. Execution at its finest.

Seeing the success of this method, a few of the other quarterbacks and receivers joined in on this action. With footballs being thrown and Cougar football players running drills in their direction, the Husky band members got smart and starting moving away from our side of the field.

Our mission was a success. We protected our turf and succeeded in keeping the enemy out. Finally, they left our half of the field and moved to their own.

Before I get to the lesson and the point of telling this story, let me preface that I do not condone bullying. I do not support using violence to solve a problem. Also, I completely support band, choir, and many other programs of the arts. This isn't a jock versus band theme. Marching bands are one of the many reasons why I love high school and college football. The pageantry, tradition, halftime shows, and fight song cheers wouldn't be possible without our talented and hardworking band teammates.

This story simply illustrates the interesting choices we make during competitive and stressful situations. Should the Husky Band have been on our side of the field during warm-ups? Probably not. Should we have run our pre-game drills directed at them? Definitely not. But, that is not the point.

The big picture of this parable is this: *Our half of the football field was a metaphor for our brain and our thoughts. The Husky Marching Band was the equivalent to the many distractions, doubts, and noise we must block out in order to be successful.*

To be a top performer, we must be mindful of our thoughts at all times.

We must find a way to QUIET THE NOISE.

This type of focus takes hard work and a great deal of practice. The best in any arena excel in this. Whether it's Serena, Brady, Jeter, or Jordan—they all developed a mental edge that filters out negativity and distractions, while channeling in either neutral or positive thoughts.

This book is a guide designed to do just that—give you the tools to master your mindset, quiet negative noise in your head, and in turn, be more clutch. The interesting fact about being clutch is that it's not doing anything extraordinary. The elite in the military, medicine, law, business, and sport know that you don't rise to the occasion, you rise to your training. The best performers treat practice time, game time, and crunch time the same, no different. Every rep is a championship rep, either by yourself, with teammates, or against an opponent (I will cover how to do this in more detail in the coming chapters).

My definition of being clutch is simply "doing what you can do normally but when it matters most." For example, a five-foot birdie putt at the Masters in Augusta, Georgia on Sunday is the same five-foot putt at a player's home course they've played a thousand times. It's the same distance, they're using the same ball, the same club, and the same stroke. The only difference is what that player allows his or her mind to think and body to feel.

Some athletes let their brain take over their body, but not in a good way. They play not to fail, instead of play to win.

In this book, you will learn how to calm your nerves, look at failure from a different perspective, and most importantly, *build your process*. The word "process" in this sense means mental and physical habits done daily. In other words, you will develop habits and rituals that you will rely on when it's time to perform.

Once you've mastered your process, you'll be more likely to

18

reach the holy grail for performance, and that is *being in a state of flow.* When you are in a flow state, there is no time. You have endless energy and creativity. There's no judgment. Being in flow sometimes is called, "being locked-in," or "having an out of body experience," like when basketball star Klay Thompson went off for thirty-seven points in one quarter, or when Brandi Chastain kicked the game-winning soccer penalty kick goal in the 1999 World Cup. When you are in flow, you can't be stopped. Your brain is almost switched off and you are operating completely *in the now*, operating unconsciously.

Hungarian psychologist and professor Mihaly Csikszentmihalyi coined the concept of flow after devoting his entire life to uncovering what he felt as a young child playing chess. As a young boy living in Hungary during the time of World War II, Csikszentmihalyi overcame the fear and uncertainty of the war through chess. He would become so consumed by his frequent chess matches that nothing else around him mattered. Csikszentmihalyi felt challenged, focused, excited, and a rush would come over him when he saw his skills improve. He felt endless energy, no sense of time, no judgment, and pure enjoyment.

Csikszentmihalyi noticed that other people around him—children and even adults—either found ways to keep their minds preoccupied with positive things, or became overly consumed by the harshness of the war. This concept of full immersion and focus fascinated him.

Because of this curiosity, Csikszentmihalyi later moved to America to study psychology and eventually called this enlightened consciousness being "in a state of flow," where creativity and energy come flowing like water or a current of electricity.

According to Csikszentmihalyi, "The happiest people spend

much time in a state of flow, the state in which people are so involved in an activity that nothing else seems to matter; the experience itself is so enjoyable that people will do it even at great cost, for the sheer sake of doing it."

Surgeons, athletes, public speakers, musicians, artists, soldiers, gardeners, card players—you name it—all experience states of flow, or being "in the zone." The aim for anyone performing a task is to unlock this power and sustain it as long as possible.

So how do we do this?

The first step is to better understand the characteristics of flow. That is what *Master Your Mindset* is designed to do. My experience as a standout multi-sport athlete in high school and college has led me to this place. I had a great deal of talent but often found that my mind sabotaged my body. Whether it was fear of failure, worrying about the opinions of others, or being overly critical of myself, my ability to unlock flow was hindered by my very own mindset.

The purpose of this book is for you to learn from my stories and experiences as an athlete and my deep curiosity in the field of high performance. My hope is that you do not just simply read this book, but **experience it** and apply these principles consistently. Highlight, circle, or underline concepts that speak to you. Write in the margins and open spaces. Give your favorite pages dog ears. Even consider dedicating a special journal specifically for your journey. If you do these things, you will harness the tools to *master your mindset* and win the most important game, the inner-game.

To help you get there, each chapter will cover one of eight topics or concepts that will help you build a system and a process specific to your needs:

Balance and Perspective (Chapter 1)
- See yourself as more than just an athlete or performer
- Learn the importance of subconscious thoughts and habits

Develop Your Process, Create Flow (Chapter 2)
- Build your process (daily and game routines) that will carry you through the season
- Trust the process and unlock the mental focus of flow

Courage (Chapter 3)
- Retool how you look at fear
- Learn from failure and develop a growth mindset

Vision (Chapter 4)
- How do you see yourself?
- How do you see your future?

Earn It (Chapter 5)
- What are you willing to sacrifice?
- You are a byproduct of your habits

Advertise (Chapter 6)
- Master your self-talk
- Visualize success as if it's already yours

Feed the Good Wolf (Chapter 7)
- Learn the life-changing effects of gratitude and servant leadership
- Expedite your growth through mentorship and investing in your personal development

Recovery (Chapter 8)
- Grind + Rest = Success
- Recovery is a requirement of flow

In each chapter, you will be given prompts and asked specific questions (look for the 🛈 icon) to help you create a daily and weekly process to succeed. You will learn how to **focus on the process, not the prize.** When you begin to **trust your process and not be consumed by the pressure,** your performance will improve, and you will increase your likelihood of being in a state of flow.

Between chapters, I feature examples and anecdotes of how individuals or characters have used their minds to help or hurt their performances. These sections are called *Mind Over Matter*. I hope you use these stories to understand how truly powerful your mind is and how to improve your self-talk. Your brain has the ability to be your biggest strength or your greatest weakness in achieving your goals.

It's Go Time

The aim of this book is simple: to give you the tools to lower your anxiety and increase your confidence to perform at your highest level. And when you fail, you will learn powerful strategies to help you reset and operate with a growth mindset.

There is a champion inside of you. It's time to unlock your inner greatness and build your best self. If you can win the inner-game, you will dominate the outer-game. For the body has limits, but the mind is limitless.

Let's go to work!

CHAPTER 1

BALANCE AND PERSPECTIVE

THE WHOLE IS EQUAL TO THE SUM OF ITS PARTS

Though we succeeded in quieting the noise versus the Husky Marching Band, we lost the game to a more talented and deep Husky football team led by one of my favorite college players of all-time, all-conference quarterback Marques Tuiasosopo. (Fun fact: We were baseball teammates one year on an all-star team.) That tough loss to UW in the Apple Cup concluded my sophomore football season at WSU.

After taking a month off, we began our off-season winter conditioning program. Each cold, dark winter day while working out, I would reflect on a subpar season, which was even darker. I didn't have a great year statistically. Though I was the starting slot receiver and punt returner the entire year, my production was down from my freshman season. Ever heard of the term "sophomore slump?" Well, I lived it.

I got stuck in a mental rut, like many performers do, who try to reenact the past. I was insecure and was constantly playing the comparison game. This mental hindrance limited my ability to just release and play free. I was too caught up worrying about what others thought of me—as a person and as an athlete. I let my coaches, teammates, fans, and even my family get in my head. I was playing to please everybody else, except myself. Because of this, my performance just wasn't at the level it was the year before. I was operating in a constant state of .

HAVE YOU EVER FELT THAT WAY? TAKE A MOMENT TO REFLECT AND WRITE DOWN ANY THOUGHTS OR FORCES IN YOUR LIFE THAT HAVE CREATED SELF-DOUBT OR WORRY.

I have a clear memory of an internal conversation I had with myself during that time. I was in my apartment, which was on campus, just two blocks up the hill from our training facility, Bohler Gym. I shared a four-bedroom apartment that overlooked the Cougar soccer field with three teammates: tight-end Mark Baldwin, all-conference kicker Drew Dunning, and my older brother, Patrick.

I was in the shower after an evening workout reflecting on my past two seasons, which were filled with insecurities, stress, and plagued with performance anxiety. I enjoyed being part of a team and loved my teammates, but most of the time I was a nervous wreck. As the water flowed down the drain, a part of me felt like I let two years go down the drain also. I knew I wasn't performing at my best and my lack of self-confidence as a football player was my biggest hurdle. While I was getting clean in the shower, I was mentally washing away my past negativity and wanted to start the year with a fresh and more committed approach.

I made a pact with myself. I remember thinking: *OK, Collin, you're an upperclassman now. You've completed two seasons, and you only have two seasons left. This is it. It's time to bring it and give everything you've got. Change is going to happen, it's going to happen now.*

I decided to make some changes that off-season to my commitment level and accountability. I even planned to change my facemask and chin strap to resemble one of my heros, Hall of Fame wide receiver Jerry Rice. *Look like the*

the greatest of all-time, play like the greatest of all-time, I thought.

I committed to my body and my craft like never before that year. I pushed myself to be in the best physical shape of my life. From lifting weights to conditioning drills to working on my receiver skills...I was a machine.

With this renewed approach and commitment, I had a fantastic off-season and spring. I led the team in receiving during spring ball, and my play earned me a spot as the starting Z wide receiver. This success carried over into summer conditioning and fall camp. I literally felt like I couldn't be covered that summer. All of the lifting weights, not missing a workout, and giving it all I had physically produced great results, especially in the controlled and comfortable environment of practice.

Finally, I was able to let loose and be myself. It felt great.

One would think that this momentum would carry over into our first game of the season and for the rest of the year. Any logical mind would assume that all of the hard work, improvement, and production in the spring and fall camp would carry over into a breakout performance in the first game of the season against the Idaho Vandals. Well you're wrong. I was a nervous wreck again. The week leading up to, the day before, and even hours before that first game, I was a bundle of nerves.

I only had one catch that game and even had a dropped pass. I didn't drop a pass the entire fall camp! Why was this different? The year that was supposed to be my breakout season ended up being just an average one. My lack of mental stability and confidence still plagued and hindered my performance. All of my physical training, conditioning, and skill work wasn't enough. Upon reflection, I realized I

27

had a physical game plan, but I didn't have a mental game plan.

Though I was a starter and productive member of the team that helped us to ten wins that season, and a Sun Bowl victory versus Purdue, my production was well below what I envisioned during the off-season. Why was this?

Here is my theory why: **I spent all of my effort on physical preparation and zero on my mental preparation.**

Have you ever studied your butt off for an exam, then showed up for the test and the questions asked were different than the ones you studied? It wasn't that you didn't work hard, you just worked hard in a different area...there were gaps in your studying process. Or are you the type of person who studies endlessly and knows the material, but you struggle to answer the questions because of test anxiety? This is the same idea with your mindset in athletics or performing.

Looking back, I now realize I didn't develop a consistent physical AND mental process. Emphasis on the mental side. Physically I was ready, but mentally I wasn't.

FILL UP THE GLASS JAR
DO THIS EXERCISE. REFLECT ON YOUR PAST YEAR AS AN ATHLETE, AND ADD UP TO 100 PERCENT IN THESE THREE AREAS:

- **SKILL WORK** – PRACTICING YOUR CRAFT AND SPECIFIC SKILLS IN YOUR SPORT (BY YOURSELF AND OTHERS). FOR EXAMPLE, IF YOU ARE A BASEBALL PLAYER, THIS WOULD INCLUDE TEAM PRACTICE, HOURS TAKING BATTING PRACTICE, HITTING OFF A TEE, DOING LONG TOSS, OR WORKING ON YOUR FIELDING

DEFENSE. ___%
- **PHYSICAL WORK** – LIFTING WEIGHTS, RUNNING, AND WORKING ON YOUR CONDITIONING. ___%
- **MENTAL WORK** – VISUALIZING, MEDITATING, ENHANCING YOUR SELF-IMAGE, DEVELOPING YOUR MENTAL PROCESS, PRACTICING AFFIRMATIONS, IDENTIFYING YOUR STRENGTHS, GOAL SETTING, ETC. ___%

While working with teams, I'll usually bring up a player and have them fill up a clear glass jar with three different colored candies, each one representing one of the different categories listed above. I have them ask their teammates to help them with this exercise and based on their teammates' feedback, they fill up the jar and stop with the appropriate amount for each category.

Each category is represented by a different candy and what percentage of their time made up each category. This is the most common breakdown when I do this exercise:

- **Skill Work** (Lemonheads): 60 percent...meaning they spent 60 percent of their year doing skill work (practicing their sport).
- **Physical Work** (Whoppers): 30 percent...meaning they spent 30 percent of their year doing physical work (lifting and conditioning).
- **Mental Work** (Hot Tamales):10 percent...meaning they spent 10 percent of their year doing mental work (improving their mindset and focus).

Usually, there are very few red Hot Tamales that end up filling the jar. However, there is the occasional player that says they put in more than 30 percent of mental work the previous year.

Typically, I say, "All right, tell me what that looks like." They often start out by saying how they set goals. I say,

"OK, tell me more." They usually find themselves searching for something else to say or provide other examples, and end up with nothing. They quickly change their answer to a much smaller number.

Most college and some high-level high school student-athletes can add watching film into this mental category, but only if they're doing it with the purpose to uncover tendencies, create confidence, and a mental edge. Some just watch film to watch film, but get nothing out of it. This approach definitely wouldn't count.

I follow up this exercise with one simple question. I ask, "What percent of being a championship athlete is *mental* versus *physical*?" Most commonly, the response is unanimous. Any team I have worked with unanimously says that it's more mental than physical.

"If this is true," I ask, "then why are you not doing more mental work?"

The typical response is: "We don't know how," or "No one has taught us."

I definitely fell into that camp in my college career. I always gave 110 percent physically but lacked the tools and tactics to exercise my brain to prepare for game competition.

I was usually relaxed and focused during practice, but I could not consistently carry the same mental approach to the games. This unfortunately is a common occurrence for athletes who underperform. There is a small percentage of gamers who have the innate ability to turn the switch on and perform at a high level on game day, but lack quality practice habits (I had a few of those teammates in my career). These types of performers are few and far between. The goal is to approach practice and games with the same level of importance and execution.

30

THE PERFORMANCE PENDULUM

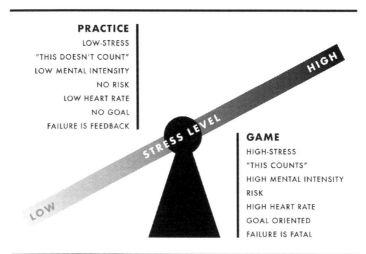

PRACTICE
LOW-STRESS
"THIS DOESN'T COUNT"
LOW MENTAL INTENSITY
NO RISK
LOW HEART RATE
NO GOAL
FAILURE IS FEEDBACK

STRESS LEVEL

HIGH

LOW

GAME
HIGH-STRESS
"THIS COUNTS"
HIGH MENTAL INTENSITY
RISK
HIGH HEART RATE
GOAL ORIENTED
FAILURE IS FATAL

IMBALANCED APPROACH

TREAT PRACTICE/GAMES/CRUNCH TIME THE SAME
HIGH MENTAL FOCUS - HIGH PHYSICAL INTENSITY
EVERY REP COUNTS - CLEAR OBJECTIVE - CONSEQUENCE BASED PLAY
TRUST YOUR PROCESS - SAME PRE-DURING-POST COMPETITION ROUTINES
PROGRESS NOT PERFECTION - PLAY IN THE NOW

STRESS LEVEL

BALANCED APPROACH

If you fall into this camp, don't worry, we are going to work on strategies to improve your mental game.

Reflecting on why my junior season was not as productive as my off-season or fall camp can be boiled down to this: I spent 50 percent on skill work and 50 percent on physical work. Though I made a commitment to give maximum effort in the off-season physically, I didn't have a system to train my brain mentally. My glass jar was filled with no Hot Tamales (mental work). I put in 0 percent for mental training, thus my performance suffered.

I didn't create a process to practice over and over again that I could rely on. I did not work on my self-image and clearly identify my strengths. I had no pre-practice or consistent pre-game routine that would reduce my stress and *decision fatigue*, which is wasted energy deciding on trivial things like what food to eat, gear to use, pre-game rituals—all of these should have been established ahead of time. Pro football quarterback Russell Wilson often says, "The separation is in the preparation." This applies to our physical and mental approach. I was not operating in a space of *unconscious competence* or flow, which is any top performer's goal. I didn't set parameters for myself or have goals while I practiced. I had no accountability measures to get comfortable playing under pressure. I rarely stepped outside my comfort zone. (I'll explain all of these concepts in more detail later.)

Here is a key fact of peak performance: *Repetition is the mother of mastery.*

If you do not simulate your workouts to emulate a game environment (playing high-tempo, having an objective, making it as challenging as possible and practicing pressure situations), it will be much harder to keep your brain out of your body's way. That was me. Without knowing the proper mental skills to utilize, I was operating in a space of *unconscious incompetence*—meaning, I didn't know that I didn't know (a mentor first explained the concepts of unconscious competence and incompetence to me, and again, we will discuss more about these concepts in just a bit).

Performance Anxiety

Can you remember a time when you had to perform in some area of your life and felt extremely nervous? Maybe it was a speech in school, asking someone out on a date, or trying out to make a select all-star team. If you felt deep stress in these moments, don't worry, feeling stressed is perfectly natural. The goal is not to be fearless, but to fear *less*. The first step is to understand that **you are not alone.**

Performance anxiety (being extremely nervous or stressed) is a real thing, and for some reason not many are talking about it, especially with young athletes and performers (drama, music, band, choir, debate, sales, etc.).

Here are some alarming stats:
- 25 percent of all teens and 30 percent of teen girls suffer from anxiety. *–Elements Behavioral Health*
- Forty million American adults (18.1 percent) suffer from anxiety. *–Anxiety and Depression Association of America* (Note: Many mental experts believe adult anxiety is under reported, and the actual number is most likely double and the percentage is into the thirties.)
- Anxiety disorders are the most common of all mental illnesses of teens. *–Elements Behavioral Health*
- 85 percent of certified collegiate athletic trainers believe that anxiety is currently an issue with student-athletes on their campus. *–NCAA.org*

I hope these numbers help normalize times when you feel stressed or nervous because of competition. No matter if you are a professional, Olympic, college, high school, or

33

youth athlete, no one is immune to feeling nervous before or during a game.

Where is the Stress Coming From?

Many performers and athletes are specializing at early ages. They are forced to juggle school and social endeavors (including dating). The pressure to perform from parents, family members, coaches, teachers, and even peers is at a very high level. This creates an endless cycle of constantly trying to make the best team, get exposure, earn a scholarship, get signed, or drafted. While balancing life outside one's sport, this process can be extremely taxing.

Instead of living up to one's potential, many athletes are living up to strenuous expectations from outside their own vision. I'm all about mentorship, coaching, and pushing yourself as far as you can go—just make sure that your actions and endeavors are on your own terms.

HOW DO YOU FEEL?

I ASK THESE THREE QUESTIONS (DEALING WITH COMPETITION) TO THE MANY TEAMS AND ATHLETES I WORK WITH. THEY DEAL WITH STRESS DUE TO COMPETITION. DO A MENTAL CHECK-IN WITH YOURSELF AND BE AS HONEST AS POSSIBLE.

1. I AM NERVOUS OR STRESSED BEFORE PERFORMING:
   A. OFTEN
   B. SOMETIMES
   C. NEVER

2. I AM NERVOUS AND STRESSED WHILE PERFORMING:
   A. OFTEN
   B. SOMETIMES
   C. NEVER

3. I UTILIZE A MENTAL AND PHYSICAL ROUTINE TO HELP LOWER
   MY FEAR AND STRESS:
   A. OFTEN
   B. SOMETIMES
   C. NEVER

Asking these questions to hundreds of athletes that I've worked with, I've found that around 90 percent say they sometimes or often times feel stressed either before or during competing in a game. However, only about 10 percent say they have developed mental and physical routines to help lower their stress.

This is where developing a process comes in. By predetermining and developing patterns and rituals done consistently before, during, and after competition, you'll naturally be in a more relaxed and focused state. Many performers lack this understanding and succumb to pressure.

Before we delve into developing your process to help deal with the pressures listed above, let's address four mental challenges that sometimes hinder performance.

Four Challenges

1. *White Matter*
   Most athletes who compete at a high level are at their peak physically. However, a main function of the brain called "white matter" is not fully formed until much later. This white matter is sometimes called the "subway of the mind" because it enables nerve signals to travel freely between different parts of the brain. White matter isn't fully formed until we are over the age of forty.

   This lack of white matter development affects one's judgment, decision-making, and the ability to deal

35

with emotions.

Also, the prefrontal cortex of the brain—which serves as the mind's filter, helps moderate social behavior, and aids in complex cognitive planning—isn't fully formed until we are twenty-one. This might help explain why I made some seriously stupid decisions as a teen (*Sorry, Mom and Dad for driving your car through our garage*) and had a tough time with failure and rejection.

2. *Balance*
Many performers receive a majority of their self-validation and self-love from how they perform (myself included). Speaking from experience, a bad performance would impact me emotionally and last for hours, days, and even weeks. If I dropped a pass, went hitless in a baseball game, or missed a bunch of shots in basketball, I'd feel like I wasn't a good person. Winning was how I felt loved.

This mindset couldn't be further from the truth. Self-confidence, success, or failure in one area of your life should not affect how you perceive yourself as a whole. You are more than just an athlete, singer, actor, musician, etc.

TAKE A MOMENT AND LIST OTHER AREAS OF YOUR LIFE THAT MAKE UP WHO YOU ARE AS A COMPLETE PERSON.

These are just as important as your role as a performer. I call this your "Me Wheel."

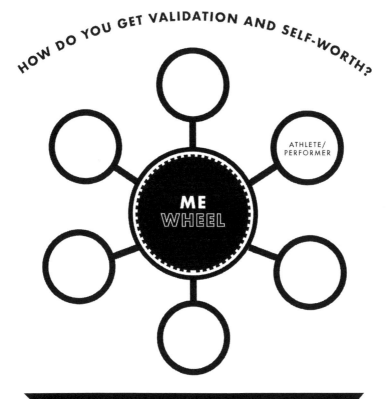

HOW DO YOU GET VALIDATION AND SELF-WORTH?

ATHLETE/
PERFORMER

ME
WHEEL

BE MORE THAN ONE THING.

3. *COPPs*
Many athletes and performers put themselves in what I call "performance jail" because of **COPPs**: Comparing, Opinions, Practice (lack thereof), and a bonus P, which is Perfection. They feel trapped and their abilities are often times held back because of these self-inflicted wounds and environmental factors.

Comparing
» Social media has added a unique layer of stress to young people and even adults these days. We often times judge our "behind the scenes" to other people's

37

highlights through likes, comments, and followers. For many people, their profile and online presence makes up a large part of their identity. This is playing with fire.

» Besides social media, playing the comparison game often impacts our confidence because of the constant judging and evaluating of other people. Trust me, the grass isn't always greener. This happens at school, work, during competition, and in life. This is an endless cycle that serves no one. Focus on what you have and your strengths, instead of wasting your energy on what you can't control—including other people's accomplishments, traits, and possessions.

» Have the mindset that when others succeed, it doesn't take away anything from your success. Cheer for others, so they can cheer for you.

Opinions
» Worrying about other people's opinions of you is a significant obstacle to creativity. Listen, it's none of your business what others think of you.

» In the end, opinions are just that—opinions. They are not facts. It only takes one—as in one scout, one coach, one team—to like you and give you an opportunity. Focus on that concept instead of stressing over pleasing everyone.

Practice
» According to Mark Mathews, one of the best big wave surfers in the world, "The only way of overcoming our fears and anxieties, is by doing that activity." Often times, stress in a particular moment is caused because we have not put ourselves in that situation enough times. Fear of failure holds us back from doing the most important element of improvement: *practicing.*

» Deliberate practice is the pathway to skill,

growth, and enjoyment. Thus, a lack of practice increases stress when faced with that task and results in a lower likelihood of success.

Perfection

» No human is perfect. However, many athletes possess an intense inner drive to be the best, which can sometimes backfire. These types of individuals give themselves no grace and oftentimes beat themselves up mentally after a mistake. In my opinion, if your focus is playing perfect, you will be overly tense and tight. With this approach, you will actually make more mistakes. Instead, switch your focus away from being perfect and more toward growth and improvement. Progress is the game, not perfection.

4. *Unconscious Incompetence*
    Have you ever heard the expression, "You don't know what you don't know?" This lack of awareness is also called "unconscious incompetence." Meaning, you are unaware of crucial information that can help you be at your best. This is a state that I was operating in for most of my college athletic career, especially my lackluster junior season. During my training, I had prepared myself physically, but not mentally. This was largely because I was not taught a framework or process to combat the challenges I listed above.

    The goal is to operate in a state of unconscious competence or in a state of flow. This is where you've rehearsed a specific act so many times, that you can perform and execute it without thinking. An example is how you drive a car. You often don't even think about all of the actions necessary to get from Point A to Point B. You've performed these tasks so many times your subconscious mind simply takes over.
    Your subconscious mind has more power than your

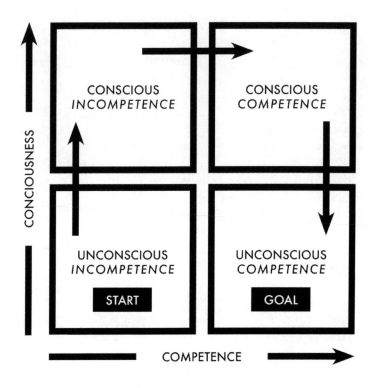

conscious mind. It is your brain's memory bank. It stores and retrieves data for you when action is needed. Your subconscious mind keeps you in a state of homeostasis by keeping you thinking and acting consistent to the way you have operated in the past. It often times keeps you in your comfort zones.

It's time to reprogram your subconscious mind to help you, not hurt you.

The next chapter will help you recognize blind spots in your preparation and give you the tools to unlock the most powerful force any athlete or performer can obtain, and that is being in a state of flow.

How do you unlock flow? By developing your own personalized process. I'll discuss both concepts in Chapter 2.

THE BANNISTER EFFECT

People said it couldn't be done. It wasn't possible. The closest any human had ever come to running under a four-minute mile was in the 1940s, with a time of 4:01. Track athletes and experts believed the human body just wasn't built to beat the four-minute mile barrier.

After a subpar showing at the 1952 Olympics, medical student and Britain's best mile runner, Roger Bannister, had a clear goal: Be the first athlete to run a mile under four minutes.

Due to his rigorous scholastic schedule studying to be a neurologist, Bannister would train his body physically by running sparingly, a simple 30-minute daily interval routine was all he needed to prepare his body. While training physically was important, his self-belief and vision made all the difference.

With this inspiring goal, the Harrow, England native would often close his eyes and visualize every step of the race. While creating this image mentally before it happened, Bannister would see the finish line, hear the roar of the crowd, and feel the excitement of making history.

What separated Bannister from the the others who failed was that he believed with all of his might that he could do it. He even placed a little piece of paper that read 3:58 in his shoe while he ran.

This belief, clear vision, and deliberate practice paid off.

On May 6, 1954, the world of track and field was forever altered. Once thought as impossible was now possible. On an overcast and windy day (which finally died down), Bannister defied the odds and ran a world record 3:59.4 mile. The crowd of more than 3,000 went wild when he crossed the finish line and his time was announced. He did it! Bannister defied what even physicians said couldn't be done. What began first in his mind and later felt in his heart became a reality.

Bannister inspired millions that day, including his rival, Australia's John Landry. Just forty-six days later, Landy beat Bannister's record. Not to be outdone, the two paired off in what was dubbed as "The Miracle Mile" in August later that year. While trailing most of the race, Bannister beat Landy on the final turn.

Bannister defied the odds again. In what seemed like a raced he couldn't win, Bannister battled back and won more from his faith than from his talent.

Bannister's goal, written in his shoe, came true. He posted a time of 3:58.8, while Landy finished just behind him with a time of 3:59.6. At that point in history, both runners had posted the top under four-minute times in the world.

For decades, people thought that breaking the four-minute mile was unbeatable, but because of Bannister's accomplishment, he inspired nearly a dozen runners to beat the four-minute mile barrier within two years of his record.

Within five years, even a high school athlete ran a sub-four-minute mile.

Here's a recap of this trailblazer's story:

- Bannister turned his 1952 Olympics failure of not medaling into fuel to improve.
- He started his training with a clear goal and visualized it occurring daily.
- Bannister broke down his goal into smaller goals including shaving each lap by a specific time.
- He carried over his discipline as an athlete into a successful career as a doctor of neurology.
- **After decades of believing something couldn't be done, Bannister inspired hundreds of track athletes to BELIEVE and BEAT the four-minute mile.**

Look at your life right now. What do you or others around you think to be impossible? Use Roger Bannister's story as an example. With a clear vision, belief, and practice, you can turn the impossible into possible…and inspire others to do the same.

CHAPTER 2

DEVELOP YOUR PROCESS, CREATE FLOW

REPEATED ACTION BECOMES INSTINCT

It was a cold, crisp February evening on the Palouse, and I had recently completed my junior football season. This off-season felt much different. Though I wasn't happy with my production that season, the team and Cougar Nation got our swagger back. We finished the season with a bowl win, and a number ten national ranking. The next season we were returning many starters, including Heisman hopeful and all-conference quarterback, Jason Gesser. I was very optimistic going into my last off-season, despite my lackluster sophomore and junior seasons statistically.

We just finished with a winter conditioning practice on Roger's Field, and while stretching with my teammates after practice, I saw Head Football Coach Mike Price begin to walk my way.

While side-stepping melting white snow on the green turf, he finally stopped right in front of me. After blowing warm breath into his cold hands a few times, he looked down beneath his huge crimson parka and said, "Great workout today huh, Collin?"

I looked back up at him after finishing my hamstring stretch and replied, "Yup Coach, we definitely got better tonight."

He nodded at me and then went right for it: "You know

what Collin, I think you should play baseball. I just talked with Coach Mooney [the head WSU baseball coach], and he said they could use another outfielder." He then concluded, "You should go talk to him. You know the playbook well enough. Your spot is safe here."

Me? Play now?, I thought. *I haven't had a live at-bat since high school.*

Stunned, I nodded my head and replied, "Sure thing, Coach. I'll go see him." While I walked back to the locker room, a pit began to form in my stomach.

Coming out of high school, I had many more scholarship offers in baseball than football. It was a more natural sport for me. I committed to WSU my senior year of high school with the intent of playing both football and baseball. However, deep down inside, I hid the fact that I really didn't enjoy baseball. The game was too slow and I was often times so hard on myself when I failed. Over time, I had lost the inner joy of playing this game that was full of failure. Instead of being a game of fun, baseball was a game of fear and anxiety for me.

After earning a starting position my freshman year in football, I only practiced with the baseball team for a month that first winter in Pullman. I knew my heart just wasn't in it. I told the coaching staff that I couldn't continue playing baseball and was going to focus 100 percent on football. In the back of my mind, I left the door open to return at some point, but for the time being, I was done.

So there I was, two years later in Coach Mooney's office, discussing whether or not I should come out of baseball retirement. You see, Coach Mooney was in a pinch. His starting right fielder tore his ACL during the season opener the week before, and his center fielder was surprisingly academically ineligible. He needed another outfielder on the roster...bad.

"I haven't had a live at-bat in about three years," I said during that meeting. "I'll come out to practice and see how it feels."

Deep down, I knew I couldn't let the Cougs down. The coaching staff and I agreed that I would turnout. And there I was...about to be a two-sport college athlete. Just the thought of that feat got me excited.

That was a Tuesday. I practiced on Wednesday and Thursday and was suited up for the first time in the Cougar pinstripes on Friday, in a weekend series versus Gonzaga University.

I remember that first Friday game watching from the dugout. I must have taken a hundred mental reps that game. With each pitch, I pretended I was at the plate. I'd watch the pitch, work on my timing, and would feel the bat hit the ball in my mind. While watching from the dugout, I kept telling myself, I *can play with these guys. Most of these players I either played with or against during select summer ball. Heck, I've got nothing to lose.*

Then I internalized, *I wonder if I'll even get to play this weekend?*

When I got to the ballpark the next morning, I was a little shocked. *What? I'm in the lineup,* I thought to myself as I saw my name penciled in the starting lineup card posted in our dugout. At that moment, I knew it was go time.

During warmups and batting practice, my mind replayed images of the weekend before at my parents' house. Growing up, my brother and friends played Wiffle ball for hours

49

in our front yard. We loved this game. We created rules and had our own way of keeping score and measuring what type of hit is was: over the fence—homerun; in the neighbor's beauty bark—a triple; in the grass—a double; hit it out of the driveway on a line—a single.

Ironically, I was home on a weekend away from Pullman just six days prior. That weekend was no different than my childhood. My brother and a few of our friends spent most of that Saturday home playing Wiffle ball. While playing, I didn't have a single thought of turning out with the baseball program that season.

So there I was exactly a week later, not playing Wiffle ball but an actual real live game. I remember thinking during warm-ups before the first pitch versus Gonzaga, *If I can hit the equivalent of a ninety mile-per-hour moving Wiffle ball, I can hit this soft lefty.*

My Friday visualization and Saturday self-talk served me well. The first pitch I saw as a Division I baseball player was a line drive base hit to right field. I finished the day with two hits and followed this initial performance with another two hits on Sunday. Batting .500 with a walk in my first two collegiate games felt amazing—especially after taking several years off. But, I wasn't done. On Monday we had a game with NAIA powerhouse Lewis and Clark State. This program gets more guys drafted than most PAC-12 teams, and they have multiple national championships. So, with my sore right arm (I hadn't thrown a baseball in more than two years) we took our university vans down the forty-five-minute drive to Lewiston, Idaho.

Staying in this loose and focused mindset, I continued my positive self-talk: *I have nothing to lose here,* I thought again. *I can use this extra practice before we start conference play. Let's just relax, play hard, and maximize these*

50

at-bats.

Often times as an an athlete, and especially a hitter, less is more. In this particular case, this "less is more" mental approach served me well. I went two-for-two with a three-run homerun and three walks that game. Several of my teammates, including our first baseman, Steve Mortimer (who later played in the Washington Nationals organization), were a little surprised, and Mortimer said, "Geez, C-Hen, you should give up football and play baseball full-time."

"Yeah right," I replied. "It's just three games," I said while trying to be humble. On our drive back up to Pullman though, I reflected on what just happened.

After taking nearly three years off, in my first three games as a college baseball player, I went six-for-ten, with a homerun and four walks. That's a .714 on-base percentage. In this brief period, while not even realizing it, I was playing in **a state of flow**—no judgment, complete inner-peace and relaxation; I was filled with energy and confidence; my self-talk and visualization was of nothing but positive outcomes; and I was living in the moment without any sense of time (past or future). And here's another key point: I was stepping outside my comfort zone and putting myself in a new challenging environment—one of the main triggers to unlock flow.

For that three-day period I felt what icons like basketball great Steph Curry and Olympic and World Champion skier Lindsey Vonn have often felt in moments of peak performance: power and rhythm like a flowing river.

It is one thing to reach full immersion and complete focus...it's another thing to sustain it.

The next weekend we competed in a series of games in a

tournament down in College Station, Texas, at Texas A&M University. I went one-for-ten in my next two games. I couldn't recreate the magic of the weekend before. We ended up winning the tournament, and I had a ninth inning game-tying single to help beat the University of Kentucky, but the fact that I lacked a constant process (mental and physical routines performed consistently), hindered my ability to continue that mental concentration.

We'll pause my story here.

CAN YOU THINK OF PERFORMANCES OR GAMES WHEN YOU WERE IN THE ZONE? REPLAY AND DESCRIBE THOSE MOMENTS AND FEELINGS NOW.

WHAT ROUTINES WERE YOU DOING BEFORE BEING IN THAT PEAK MENTAL STATE?

The rest of this chapter will explore how to increase your likelihood of being in a flow state (similar to the one I just described) by developing a process.

Process First, Flow Second
The term "trust the process" has been more and more commonly used in the field of athletics as a blueprint of success. Legendary college football coach Nick Saban has stressed the importance of coaching up the process. One of the reasons why Saban and the University of Alabama Crimson Tide have been so dominant the past decade—with multiple conference championships, national titles, and top recruiting classes—is because he coaches process, not outcomes.

He understands the simple fact that as flawed humans,

we can't control outcomes. We can't control our statistics, numbers, opinions, and rankings. The Alabama program is built on this simple philosophy: *Though we can't control outcomes, we can control our process—our commitments, our routines, and our habits.* Why is this important? It's simple, if your habits and routines are of a championship caliber, the results will come.

University of Minnesota Head Football Coach P.J. Fleck agrees. While leading his previous program, Western Michigan University, to a conference championship, multiple bowl games—including a Cotton Bowl appearance—he often stressed to his players to focus on the process, not the prize. Fleck understands the unproductive path of being seduced by accolades and playing for praise instead of competing to be your best self.

Another example is the entire Philadelphia 76ers basketball organization, which has adopted the mantra of "Trust The Process" for their plan to rebuild and become a winning program again and for competing each night.

Having a process comes down to creating a preemptive plan for yourself. Life, and especially sports, are so unpredictable. In the field of competition, sometimes it's just not your night. Or the player you are facing is playing out of his or her mind. No player or team can sustain perfection forever—even the mighty UConn women's basketball team knows this (the Huskies broke their three-year winning streak in 2017).

The better you develop a plan, hone in on your process and routines, the better you will play. And most importantly, have a system that you can replicate for future success.

HERE ARE SOME QUESTIONS TO CONSIDER:

- DO YOU CREATE A LONG-TERM PLAN ON HOW YOU WILL PRACTICE AND PREPARE FOR THE SEASON?
- WHAT ARE YOUR ROUTINES RIGHT NOW?
- DO YOU HAVE THE SAME PRE-GAME ROUTINE?
- ARE YOU UTILIZING THE SAME GEAR AND EQUIPMENT IN PRACTICE AS YOU ARE IN GAMES?
- WHAT ARE YOUR WEEKLY AND DAILY RITUALS AS YOU PREPARE FOR COMPETITION?
- HOW MUCH SLEEP ARE YOU GETTING EACH NIGHT?
- WHAT ARE YOU EATING AND DRINKING? GARBAGE LIKE PROCESSED FAST FOOD, OR HEALTHIER MEALS?
- HAVE YOU MADE A MUSIC PLAYLIST THAT YOU CONSISTENTLY LISTEN TO BEFORE GAMES?
- HOW ARE YOUR PRACTICE HABITS?
- IS THERE A CONSEQUENCE IF YOU DO NOT EXECUTE IN PRACTICE?

When you have practiced these routines many times over, the natural byproduct is a more relaxed and comfortable state. You'll be in that mindset of unconscious competence—performing without thinking—like the example of driving a car over and over again. Athletics and other channels of competition are no different.

The goal is to ingrain these rituals into your subconscious, so they become automatic. Thus, when it's time to perform—no matter if it is a practice or a game—you will have rehearsed these mental and physical actions so many times that you let your subconscious take over and just release and play at your best.

You want to avoid *decision fatigue*, which I briefly mentioned is wasting your brain energy on things that do not matter. Instead, you want all of your energy focused on what you need to do to play at your best. There's a reason why Barack Obama wore only gray and navy suits each day. He wanted to focus his energy and brain power on being the best president he could be—and not on what he was going to wear. Facebook founder Mark Zuckerburg also has a similar approach. He conserves his mental energy by wearing a similar style of gray t-shirt everyday.

HAVE YOU PREDETERMINED WHAT GEAR, EQUIPMENT, AND CLOTHING YOU ARE GOING TO WEAR FOR PRACTICE AND GAMES?

I've said it before and I'll say it again: **Repeated actions become instinct.** This could be a good or a bad thing based on your mental and physical habits. Let's discuss a winning strategy that will improve your likelihood of unlocking your subconscious, operating in a state of flow, and being more clutch.

Four Keys on the Power of Process
Treat all of these scenarios the same:
1. Training by yourself
2. Practicing with teammates
3. Game time
4. Crunch time

Training by yourself – Have goals and accountability measures while you are working on your craft alone. With these measurable goals, have a consequence if they are not attained. Part of unlocking flow is operating in a state of risk. You must develop your clutch muscle by practicing under pressure. The more you can operate under these parameters, the better you'll become. Navy SEALs follow this creed. There are consequences in battle, thus with every training exercise, they create consequences (punishment or reward) for winning or losing.

> *Example* – While performing shooting drills in basketball, have a goal of how many shots you must make out of a predetermined number. For every one you miss, run a set of lines. Or make conditions more challenging on yourself—wear a weighted vest; use a smaller, larger, or heavier ball (depending on your sport); push yourself to accomplish a challenging number of reps in a limited amount of time. If you do not achieve your goal, create a consequence. These techniques will make competition with others easier.

Practicing with teammates – A key ingredient to Seahawks Head Coach Pete Carroll's winning ways is his core belief: *Always Compete.* Meaning, compete the same during practice as you do in a game. If you've ever seen a Seahawks practice, you've witnessed the tempo, energy, and sense of urgency no matter if it's during individual drills, one-on-ones, or team competition. They are at a level ten at all times. Carroll's practice philosophy has paid off well, which is evident by his multiple national championships at USC and being a Super Bowl champion in the NFL. If you can bring a high level of intensity during practice, and approach these individual and team competitions with the same mindset and effort as you do for games, this will help with your nerves and execution when it's game time.

> *Example* – Your approach with practice shouldn't be any different than how you treat games. Set goals for specific accomplishments you can measure during practice. Wear and use the same gear and equipment in practice as you do in games. Warm up the same. Refine your techniques and reinforce your fundamen-

DEVELOP YOUR PROCESS, CREATE FLOW

tals. Keep score and have a repercussion with every drill and competition. Establish pre-practice, pre-game, and pre-play routines mentally and physically—keep these consistent. This repetition will serve you when it's game day. Remember: TREAT PRACTICE AND GAMES THE SAME! This approach will increase your likelihood of performing at a high level of *unconscious competence.*

Game time – Let your winning habits take over and trust the process. No one did this better than the great Yankee shortstop Derek Jeter. Jeter was known as "The Captain" or "Captain Clutch." His relentless focus was evident no matter the season or game. Jeter even moved to Tampa, Florida to be near the Yankees' training facility so he could hone in on his craft year round. What's unique about this Yankee legend was his consistency. Though he was known as a clutch player, his batting average in spring training, the regular season, and post-season were nearly identical (all over .300). By sticking to his routines, and having the same approach no matter if it was taking hacks in Tampa, on an away series in early summer, or if it was deep into November, every game and practice was a championship game. This focus paid off for the all-time Yankees and MLB post-season hits leader.

> *Example* – Rehearse your preparation and execution during practice relentlessly—then carry over the same approach during game day. Use the same warm-up routine. Wear the same gear. Utilize the same pre-play self-talk and physical rituals. Once it's game day, instead of focusing on the pressure to perform or on the outcomes, go back to your practice rituals and trust them. If you haven't put in this work, you'll be able to feel it, and the lack of production will show. If you did put in the work, then simply trust the process, compete like heck, and have fun. If you've put in the time

57

to let your habits form, you'll position yourself to more likely be in a state of flow—less thinking and more just playing. Finally, set a measurable objective or goal for the game. This will give your mind purpose and clarity to perform at your best.

Crunch time – After Kobe Bryant's historic sixty-point performance during his final game as a Laker, a reporter asked him a question along the lines of: "Kobe, with the world watching, and everyone knowing this is your final game, how did you do it? You even hit the game-winning shot." The Black Mamba took a sip from his sports drink and said that he kept to his routine. He didn't change a thing with his pre-game preparation and focus during the game...even down the final stretch. The five-time world champion noted that there were a few moments when he got caught up in the hype, and during these moments, his shot got cold. However, he said when he got back to his process, and quit judging his performance, the baskets and his rhythm came back to him.

Treat crunch time or last-second moments the same as all the other examples I've previously listed. These actions are the same as any other—the only difference is not allowing your mind to make them bigger. In the end, always go back to your routines, and remember this statement when you're training and during clutch time: WE DON'T RISE TO THE OCCASION, WE RISE TO OUR TRAINING. This statement rings true in the military, sales, medicine, the arts, school, and sports. If you've put yourself in pressure situations during practice, you'll find that the frequency of coming through in the clutch will be much higher.

Example – While lining up to kick the field goal of his life, New York Giants kicker Lawrence Tynes was facing some tough conditions. It was the NFC Championship Game, and there were merely seconds left on

58

the clock. The Giants were trailing on the road in the hostile frozen tundra of Lambeau Field—the home of the favored Green Bay Packers. If Tynes were to make this kick, he would send his team to the Super Bowl. If he missed, their season would be over.

There was a problem, though. Earlier in the game, Tynes shanked two field goals, and with the conditions nearing below zero, many wondered if it was even physically possible to make this kick. So after the Packers called a timeout to "ice" him (literally), Tynes lined up for the kick. He did his measured steps, set his feet, looked up at the holder, and nodded his head. The snap was placed, the kick was up...and...he drilled it. "The Giants are going to the Super Bowl!" yelled the TV commentator. During post-game interviews, Tynes was asked what he was thinking before making that kick—especially after badly missing his two previous attempts. Similar to Kobe, Tynes replied that he didn't change a thing. He stuck to his routine.

Are you seeing a theme here? In stressful and crucial times, it's perfectly normal to be nervous. However, instead of allowing your mind to think about what would happen if you fail, focus your energy on the habits and rituals that got you there. If you trust your process, you will be more likely to finish in clutch fashion like Jeter, Kobe, and Tynes.

BUILD YOUR PROCESS

PULL OUT A PIECE OF PAPER (OR JOURNAL) AND START CREATING CONSISTENT ROUTINES FOR YOUR:

- PHYSICAL PLAN TO IMPROVE STRENGTH, EXPLOSION, AND SPEED
- MENTAL FITNESS PLAN (VISUALIZATION, PRACTICING MIND-FULNESS, GOAL SETTING, POSITIVE AFFIRMATIONS, ETC.)
- HEALTHY MEAL AND HYDRATION PLAN, ESPECIALLY FOR THE WEEK OF, THE DAY BEFORE, AND DAY OF YOUR GAME
- PRE-GAME MUSIC PLAYLIST
- CLEAR OBJECTIVE SET FOR YOURSELF AND FOR THE GAME
- GEAR, UNDER CLOTHES, AND EQUIPMENT YOU PLAN TO WEAR FOR PRACTICE AND GAMES
- WARM-UP ROUTINE FOR PRACTICE AND GAMES
- "PRE-PLAY" ROUTINE; EXAMPLES:
  - » BASEBALL: HAVE A BATTER'S BOX ROUTINE (CLEAR THE DIRT, TAKE A BREATH, AND LOOK AT THE LABEL ON THE BAT), AND HAVE ONE SWING THOUGHT (E.G., "HANDS BACK"). HAVE A PHYSICAL ROUTINE BEFORE EACH PITCH ON DEFENSE, ALSO.
  - » BASKETBALL: HAVE A FREE THROW ROUTINE, AS WELL AS ONE SHOT THOUGHT (E.G., "HAND UNDER THE BALL").
  - » FOOTBALL: KNOW YOUR PRE-SNAP READS AND SELECT ONE OR TWO KEYS TO FOCUS ON.
  - » VOLLEYBALL: HAVE A SERVE ROUTINE AND ONE MENTAL KEY ON DEFENSE.
- POST-GAME ROUTINE (ICE, STRETCH, JOURNAL, WATCH FILM, ETC.)

When you develop and commit to these rituals, you will feel your stress diminish and confidence improve. You will create a sense of comfort while performing these routines. Your energy and focus will be more on your process versus worrying about who's in the stands, what would happen if

60

you fail, or what people are going to say about you behind your back, at school, on Twitter or Instagram.

As we continue to better understand how to unlock flow, the next chapter will discuss an important element of becoming your best self...and that is getting comfortable being uncomfortable by having one of the most important traits of success: **courage**.

MENTAL HEALTH

According to Lissa Rankin, MD, who runs an integrative medicine practice and is the author of the book *Mind Over Medicine,* "The key to remember is how our minds feel as we go about our day—how relaxed, happy, and fulfilled we are—gets translated into the physiology of the body."

That's why she says sometimes healthy people make themselves sick or under perform because of their thoughts and beliefs.

Do you know any of these people?

We can tap into the power of the mind to feel better or worse.

Here is an example I learned from Russell Wilson's mental performance coach, Trevor Moawad (who has also done mental coaching for national championship programs like Alabama and Florida State). These story highlights are from a 1978 edition of the magazine *Success Unlimited,* which featured an article written by Dr. Harold R. McAlindon called, *You Can if You Believe You Can—Reflections on Human Potential:*

• In Russia, a railway employee accidentally locked himself in a refrigerator car and couldn't get out.

- He started writing sentences on the wall of the car as he became colder and his body became numb. He wrote: "Slowly freezing to death...I can hardly write...These may be my last words."
- Though he was found dead, the temperature of the car was actually fifty-six degrees because the freezing mechanism was out of order. In reality, there was no physical reason for his death.
- The employee was the victim of deception created in his mind—his mind told his body that he was freezing to death, and his mind won.
- Our minds are powerful and capable of creating the future. Never underestimate the power of your mind.

ARE YOUR THOUGHTS HURTING OR HELPING YOU PERFORM AS YOUR BEST SELF?

CHAPTER 3

COURAGE

COURAGE COMES BEFORE CONFIDENCE

That first baseball season was quite the year for me. I experienced firsthand what two-sport athletes like Bo Jackson and Deion Sanders went through in college. I was juggling school, strength training, traveling two weekends a month, playing baseball, and incorporating more than five weeks of spring football.

I'll never forget my first two-sport Saturday as a Division I athlete. It was our first football scrimmage of the spring. Warm-ups in Martin Stadium began at 9:30 a.m., and our full-contact scrimmage started at 10 a.m. I remember having a productive game. I had several catches and helped the offense move the ball down the field. But I couldn't finish the scrimmage. I left our inner-squad game early because we had a 2 p.m. baseball game versus our conference foe, the Arizona State University Sun Devils.

On these Saturdays, I would leave the football field and briskly jog to the football locker room. I then would take my pads off, unwrap the tape from my wrists, cut off my taped ankles, and leave for the baseball locker room. There I would change into my Cougar pinstripes and head to Bailey-Brayton Field. Those were my favorite weekends.

I had a solid year that season on the diamond. I was the starting right fielder all year and made significant contributions to the program. I hit .321 in conference play and my favorite game came in our second-to-last series of the season.

We were playing the University of Arizona in the beautiful desert of Tucson. On this hot May weekend, we finished Saturday with a 1-1 tie in the series. Sunday was the rubber match and the winner would take the series.

I remember waking up that Sunday morning feeling horrible physically. I don't know if it was because I ate something that didn't settle right or if I was dehydrated. I'm guessing the latter. I played basketball all day Saturday with my close childhood friend, Jason Johnson (who was also Arizona's record-setting starting quarterback). Wow, the stupid things we do when we're young. After struggling to eat breakfast, I got on the bus that morning not knowing if I had enough strength to play.

When we arrived at the ballpark, I remember thinking to myself, *OK, Collin, listen to a few songs on your headphones, run a few laps around the warning track, and see how you feel.*

So off I went. With each step hitting the red, rocky warning track dirt, while listening to Usher, I gained strength. I aided my resilience by giving myself affirmations saying, *You got this. You can do it. You'll be fine. Let's go for it.*

After my run, I decided I could overcome being physically ill and play.

To enhance my focus and determination, I wrote down "You got this" on my left taped wrist and planned on touching it if I felt sick or didn't have energy.

This strategy worked. I went 4-4, with five RBIs, including an epic final at-bat.

68

Now, I'm not saying I was like Michael Jordan in his famous 1997 NBA Finals flu game, but I remember feeling horrible and needing extra mental toughness and grit to get through the extremely hot conditions, my lack of energy, and feeling physically sick.

My final at-bat was like an out of body experience. I was truly in a flow state, which was good because it was the ninth inning with two outs, we were down two runs, and the bases were loaded. These are the kind of scenarios you dream of as a young ball player.

Even though I was behind in the count, I didn't panic or worry. I felt relaxed and had total focus. With a 2-2 count, I ripped a double to right field and cleared the bases, which gave us a one-run lead that we held in the bottom of the ninth inning. To finish with the game-winning hit felt better than winning the lottery. I remember cheering with my teammates, high-fiving, hugging, and celebrating like we were in little league. That is the beauty of sport. Coming together as a team. That was my favorite moment from that season.

This next part, however, is where I reveal the not-so-good stuff.

Our final series of the season was on the road again, this time in Palo Alto versus the storied Stanford Cardinal. With that previous four-hit performance, my overall batting average for the season jumped up to .311 (I'm not sure what my conference average was, but it was much higher at that time).

Before the series I calculated that I only needed to go one-for-seven to keep my overall season batting average above .300. Talk about lowering your standards. I was allowing myself to get seduced by the numbers, to focus too much on statistics. This is what I call "focusing on the fruit and not the root." As athletes, we can't always control outcomes and stats (the fruit), but we *can* control our attitude, concentration, and effort (the root).

FRUIT

WE CAN'T CONTROL:
OPINIONS, OUTCOMES, STATS, ACCOLADES, MEDIA

ROOT

WE CAN CONTROL:
HABITS, ROUTINES, PROCESS, VALUES, COMMITMENTS, TEAM-FIRST MINDSET

With this fear of failure mindset, I went hitless the entire series, and my final season average dropped just below .300. Not finishing strong really affected me. I felt more sick to my stomach than I did the week before versus Arizona, when I was physically ill. All I wanted to do was finish the year hitting above .300, but I approached that final series like a coward. I focused solely on my individual performance and lacked the perspective of looking at that weekend from a team perspective, asking how I could contribute.

My lack of courage—not trusting the process but fearing

success as much as failure—really impacted my performance. To make matters worse, Stanford swept the series.

The rest of this chapter focuses on helping you develop your courage muscle, which is one of the first and most crucial steps to becoming more clutch and operating in flow.

Get Out of Your Comfort Zone
There are three zones we operate in as performers:
1. Comfort zone
2. Stretch zone (*FLOW*)
3. Panic zone

While studying performance psychology and successful people, one thing is clear: The greats are able to have the courage to step outside their comfort zones and tackle new challenges. Whether it's learning a new skill, trying a new system, or facing a better opponent—challenging the status quo is a must to increase the likelihood of unlocking the power of performing in a flow state.

Comfort and panic zones are unhealthy places in which to consistently operate. According to Seattle Mariners Hall of Fame Manager Lou Piniella, the key is to "Get comfortable being uncomfortable."

According to flow researchers, including Steven Kotler, the director of research at the Flow Genome Project, the aim is to stretch yourself just above your ability. When you set stretch goals, and operate in slightly uncharted territory for yourself (Kotler and colleagues suggest at least 4 percent), you unleash natural performance enhancers: norepinephrine, dopamine, endorphins, anandamide, and serotonin. All five affect performance, including increased focus, energy, learning, pain tolerance, and joy.

When you play it safe and live in your comfort zone, you are doing your performance, potential, and ability a disservice.

Playing opponents or performing tasks that are not challenging will not improve your skills or unlock flow. For example, playing the first level of a video game gets boring fast. Conversely, signing up to compete in a video game tournament when you've never played the game before might set you into panic mode. According to the godfather of flow, Dr. Mihaly Csikszentmihalyi, a hack to unlock this heightened state is to find the sweet spot that is right above your skill set, but not too far where it sets you over the edge with anxiety.

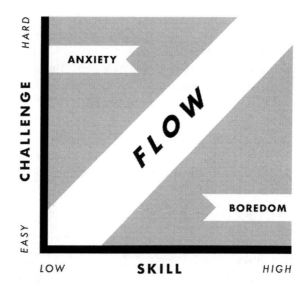

Here's the point: Make it a daily habit to do at least one thing that makes you uncomfortable and develop the courage muscle inside of you.

WHAT'S ONE AREA IN YOUR LIFE YOU CAN STRETCH YOUR COMFORT ZONE? THIS ACT IS THE ONLY WAY YOU'LL IMPROVE YOUR SKILLS AND CONFIDENCE.

Stretch Zone Ideas
Below is a list of examples to practice stretching your comfort zones:
- Wear a funky outfit (different than your normal attire) out in public.
- Volunteer for public speaking opportunities.
- Make an effort to introduce yourself to new people often.
- Address a damaged relationship.
- Try new things and learn new talents (e.g., cooking, playing an instrument, learning a new language).
- Start a blog or vlog.
- Guys, grow a mustache for a week.
- Ladies, wear your hair in a different style.
- Write a poem and share it with someone.

What other ways can you think of to stretch your comfort zones? As long as you do not put yourself or others in danger, try as many ways to grow your courage muscle as possible.

Fear
You can't have courage without fear being present. Danger is real, but fear's origin is often in our own mind.

Fear is a physical response to a mental threat. This is part of our evolutionary make-up. Luckily, we don't have to run away from sabertooth tigers for our survival anymore. Oftentimes though, when we are faced with stressful situations, our body is reacting to an event envisioned in our mind that hasn't even happened yet. A few examples: You

73

begin to take a test and your mind starts racing. You are about to ask your crush out on a date, and your palms and armpits begin to sweat profusely. You're about to give a speech, and you can't stop your heart from pounding. You're about to step on the field before a big game, and you can feel butterflies in your stomach.

These are examples of the effects of anticipation. As performers, we can use these natural chemicals and bodily reactions as a headwind that holds us back, or a tailwind that pushes us forward. Here are two real world examples of reactions to this type of anticipation (I'll mix new school with old school):

You may have heard of Zayn Malik from the musical group One Direction (1D). The group broke up, but at one point, this British boy band was one of the top grossing acts in the world, selling millions of records and selling out arenas and stadiums. While going solo, however (Malik was the first to leave the band), Malik often suffered from serious bouts of performance anxiety. His mental and physical reaction reached such a negative state, it forced him to cancel performances.

"I just couldn't go through with it," Malik told Time Magazine. "Mentally, the anxiety had won. Physically, I knew I couldn't function. I would have to pull out."

With this example, the physical reaction of anticipating worst-case scenarios, judgment, and the pressures of performing forced Malik's body to break out into a sweat, his heart rate to spike, his breathing pattern to increase, and his body to transform into an altered state. Malik used these bodily changes as a signal to back out of performing.

Don't feel bad if you have experienced a similar reaction when placed in a position where you have to perform—

we've all been there (I have felt these reactions more times than I'd like to admit).

Conversely, 1980s rock royalty, Bruce Springsteen (a.k.a., "The Boss"), sees these bodily changes as a signal that he's ready to perform. He channels the energy of an increased heartbeat. He uses the butterflies to increase his focus; he allows the natural chemicals that are released in the body (endorphins, norepinephrine, dopamine) to help him put on the performance of his life. Springsteen says that once he feels his body change this way, he knows he is ready to go out on stage and kill it.

Like The Boss, having courage is releasing the fear and channeling its power to be used as a fire that propels us forward...and not letting its heat consume us and burn us down. It's not letting your butterflies take over, but getting them in formation to help attack the moment with enthusiasm and energy.

WHAT IS YOUR THOUGHT PATTERN WHEN YOU FEEL YOUR BODY ALTER ITS STATE BECAUSE OF PRESSURE SITUATIONS?

Please note: *Consult with a medical and/or licensed mental professional if your anxiety reaches a place that jeopardizes your mental and physical health.*

No matter if it's Malik, Springsteen, Adele, or Odell Beckham, Jr., no one is immune to fear. It's perfectly normal to experience nervousness and self-doubt. However, true warriors feel the fear but go to battle anyway. Luckily for most athletes and performers (excluding extreme sports), competing isn't a life or death situation. Understand that courage comes before confidence. Often, just ten seconds of bravery facing your fear is often times all it takes...because on the other side of fear lies our deepest desires and our greatest opportunities for growth.

Face it, Bounce Back, and Learn

Reflecting on my career, the number one hindrance of performing at my best came down to one simple factor: I feared failure more than I enjoyed winning. Instead of focusing on making the play, I often would have the internal dialogue of Don't strike-out. Don't fumble the punt. Don't miss the shot.

The brain doesn't recognize the word "don't." It only pictures the event you are avoiding, thus attracting that very outcome. Operating in a mental state of worst-case scenarios and catastrophizing the future will most definitely put you in performance jail—a place where I often found myself my sophomore and junior football seasons (and often times early in my sales career). This approach makes your muscles tense and tight. Instead, get your mind and your body into a place that feels loose and light. I know it's easier said than done.

Courage and confidence don't just magically happen. Like many skills, it takes practice. A key step, that is proven to lower the stress chemical cortisol, is deep controlled breathing. In moments you find your heart rate elevating, put your hand over your stomach and focus on your breath instead of what negative things might happen. Feel your diaphragm expand. Think about your process and your purpose. Many successful athletes perform this exercise, including Team USA Olympic gold medal-winning gymnast, Laurie Hernandez (who puts a hand on her stomach, breathes deeply, and even whispers the words "I got this," especially before she competes in an event).

While you are getting re-centered with your breath, have a

visual cue to help you reset your focus. It could be some-thing in the field of competition, your gear, a teammate, or sign in the arena, field, court, or gym. These types of routines will help get your mind off of yourself and possible future mistakes.

Once you have control over your breathing and lock in on your "reset" visual, here is a three-step approach to not allow worry to overtake your conscious and unconscious mind. I call it **FBL: Face it, Bounce back, and Learn**. Use this framework to attack fear (actions, situations, or past failures you've been avoiding).

Face it
World famous actor Will Smith said that his life didn't change for the better until he got fed up with being afraid and learned how to attack his fears.

From multi-platinum rap album sales, to winning Grammy and Emmy awards, to blockbuster films, and working his way to being one of the highest paid actors in the history of Hollywood, Smith makes it look easy. But behind the glitz and glamour lies a great deal of courage and an insane work ethic.

"Ninety percent of the time, I'm uncomfortable and uncer-tain about making a movie," Smith said in an interview. "I don't want people to know how difficult it is. I think it's part of my job to make sure the audience doesn't know and they only experience the joy of the process when they see me on screen."

Smith discovered that if you do what you fear the most, there's nothing you cannot do. Our greatest promise lies within our deepest pain. From starting a sitcom, *The Fresh Prince of Bel-Air,* to starring in big-budget films like *Men in Black,* to becoming a movie producer, part of Smith's suc-

77

cess comes from his ability to stretch his comfort zone.

What Smith figured out—and what I want you to understand is—to be your best self, you can't run away from fear, but you must learn how to attack it. Start with small doses and grow from there. Often times, it's not as bad as you think. And the more you do something that once scared you, the easier it becomes.

Bounce Back
Did you know that in his first professional baseball season at shortstop, New York Yankees legend Derek Jeter (a favorite example of mine) set a minor league record of fifty-six errors? Often times his erratic arm and lack of fielding fundamentals would get the best of him. Upper management even discussed moving him to the outfield. The fact that Jeter is a first ballot Hall of Famer has less to do with his talent and more about his passion and perseverance (also known as grit). He didn't let that particular failure define him. That off-season, he worked with an infielder instructional coach every day to improve his skills. This resilience payed off in a major way. Jeter later went on to win fourteen all-star selections and five Gold Glove awards in the major leagues.

Whether you strike out, miss a tackle, get a bad grade, miss a pass, get beat on defense, or do something embarrassing in front of your peers, remember to hit the reset button and move on.

Reset Button
To help individuals and teams remember to reset, I either give them a poker chip and write "RESET" on the front. Or I hand out a silicone bracelet that says "RESET, REFOCUS, RISE." This is a physical reminder to help them reset when they make a mistake.

78

Here's some advice for you when you fail. Before you take action follow these three steps:

1. Take at least one deep breath, calm yourself, and **reset**. Flush the mistake. You can't go back and relive that moment. Like a video game, start fresh by pressing the metaphorical reset button (come up with a metaphorical or physical "button" to push, like the bracelet or poker chip example I gave above).

2. Before you take action, **refocus** your thoughts. Have a refocus ritual. Soccer legend Brandi Chastain would adjust her ponytail after a mistake. This exercise helped her calm down and refocused her mindset. Lake Chastain, remember to make sure you get your mind right before you take action. It will not help if you act out of anger, retaliation, and fear. Once you are clear mentally, it's time to use that mistake to grow.

3. Finally, use failure and adversity not to hold you down, but to fuel you to learn, improve, and **rise**. What is a good story without an obstacle to overcome? Use challenges to bring out your inner champion. I often say, "No pressure, no diamond."

An all-star select baseball team I spoke to took this message to heart. When they weren't performing well as a team, all of them tapped their reset buttons (red poker chips), to refocus their energy. For example, in one game, they were hitless after three innings of play. To help them reset, one player told everyone to hit his reset button in the dugout. What happened next was amazing—they went off to score twenty runs in that game. The team said this trick helped them win their district and regional tournament also.

When things don't go as planned, remember to reset and bounce back.

Learn
It's time you retool how you look at failure. The word FAIL stands for: First Attempt In Learning. It's important not to allow mistakes to overtake your confidence.

79

Longtime chairman and CEO of IBM computers, Thomas J. Watson, once said, "If you want to increase your success rate, double your failure rate."

Does this sound backwards to you? It might. The point is, if you are willing to go for it, with the goal of improving instead of judging on the subjective measuring tool that is a win or a loss, you will no doubt improve at a faster clip. Wins are important, but learning and improving is more important. This mindset also offers a double win. When improvement is your top aim, you tend to be less stressed and actually perform better.

The inventor of the light bulb, Thomas Edison, echoed this philosophy, but at a much higher level. With more than ten thousand attempts to discover the engineering of electricity, Edison famously said, "I have not failed. I've just found ten thousand ways that didn't work."

Whether in science, art, or sports, failure is just feedback. It doesn't define you. Be like quarterback Tom Brady in the 2017 Super Bowl and learn from an early interception and twenty-five-point deficit. Or when the Cleveland Cavaliers (basketball) and Chicago Cubs (baseball) both came back after being down 1-3 in their respective 2016 series finals. Bounce back without judgment, but from a place of learning. Regroup and compete like crazy to fight your way back.

Success should not be defined by Ws and Ls (wins and losses), but in Gs and Es (growth and effort). Because in the end, your opponent isn't the real opponent. Your real opponent is competing against yourself.

If you can apply the following quote from world-changing leader Nelson Mandela, I see a bright future in your horizon: "I never lose," he said, "I either win or I learn."

80

Fear Exercise

The higher the level of competition, the more driven the player. Often times as athletes, we are the hardest on ourselves. During these moments of feeling stress, fear, and self-doubt, tell yourself this: "If X happens (i.e., *I make a mistake, like dropping the ball*) **it really wouldn't be that bad because...**" At this point, run through a list of more rational realities. Below are examples of healthy internal dialogues after failure:

- *Everyone messes up every now and then. Even the great ones like Aaron Rodgers, Jennie Finch, and Robinson Cano fail from time to time.*
- *My teammates and coaches won't think less of me.*
- *I'll get another opportunity.*
- *The world isn't going to end.*
- *Mistakes are part of the game.*
- *Failure is feedback. What can I learn from it?*
- *I'm not defined by one play...but how I respond.*
- *As long as I went hard and competed with maximum effort, I can forgive a physical mistake. Was this a mental or physical error?*
- *There's more to me than just being an athlete.*
- *In five to ten years, no one will remember anyway.*
- *I have grace for other people when they mess up. I deserve grace, too.*

This simple exercise of walking through your fear with a more practical perspective will help you better embrace the challenges in front of you.

Growth Mindset

Stanford Psychologist Dr. Carol Dweck discovered a breakthrough concept in the field of failure and achievement. Based on her decades of research in psychology, she identified two opposing mindsets that many performers (and

81

people in general) fall into. She calls them a "fixed mind-set" and a "growth mindset." Dweck's research has been well covered in a plethora of other performance books and literature, but just in case you are not familiar with her research, let me share some key points.

According to Dweck, people's internal theories about intelligence and skill have a profound influence on their motivation to learn and improve. Individuals with a "fixed" mindset are mainly concerned with how skilled they look—they prefer tasks they can already do well and avoid ones in which they may make mistakes and not look as skilled. In contrast, she says people who believe in an *expandable* or growth mindset challenge themselves to increase their abilities, even if they fail at first.

An individual with a fixed mindset:
- Believes skill is fixed
- Seeks validation
- Avoids challenges
- Gives up easily
- Sees effort as fruitless
- Avoids or ignores feedback
- Feels threatened by others' success

Individuals with a fixed mindset tend to blame others, make excuses, and see failure as a stressful experience. Their mastery of a task is a direct correlation of how they feel about themselves. A fixed mindset individual would say, "In order to be a good person and receive love, I must perform well." These individuals constantly feel the need to prove themselves.

Reflecting back on my first collegiate baseball season—going into that final series versus Stanford—my fixed mindset hindered my performance. I spent too much energy focusing on an arbitrary number (my batting average) and felt

82

I needed to hit above .300 to validate myself. This added pressure backfired and I underperformed.

The added pressure of operating with a fixed mindset is an unhealthy place to live. If this is you, try to identify the source or the origin of this feeling or thought process. You might need to have a crucial conversation with people in your life that have modeled this to you or make you feel this way. This could be a parent, coach, teammate, or someone influential in your life.

For example, one time in college, I felt I needed to tell my dad that his intensity and behavior after I had a bad game not only made me resent him, but it took the joy out of the game. This added stress often times made me play worse. We had a heartfelt conversation and came out of it closer and with a better understanding of each other's perspective. It was uncomfortable, but necessary.

IS THERE ANYONE CLOSE TO YOU THAT IS ADDING UNWANTED PERFORMANCE STRESS IN YOUR LIFE?

If so, I encourage you not to hold it in, but to talk to somebody about it. It's beneficial for your happiness and performance to make sure that your relationships with key people in your life are positive. People cannot argue with your feelings.

Now let's look at the opposite of a fixed mindset. Growth mindset individuals do not see failing as failure, but as a learning opportunity. Not feeling this constant need to feel validated, they seek to improve their skills. This is wanting to get *better* versus feeling the need to *prove* one's self. These individuals believe that their skill isn't fixed, but can improve with time, effort, and practice.

CAN YOU THINK OF ANY TEAMMATES THAT QUIT EASILY WHEN THEY ARE TASKED WITH A CHALLENGING OPPONENT, DRILL, OR FAILURE EARLY IN COMPETITION? THEY MAKE EXCUSES OR GIVE UP EARLY TO AVOID THE EMBARRASSMENT OR PERCEPTION THAT THEY ARE NOT GOOD. DOES THIS SOUND LIKE YOU?

If this is you, work on operating with a growth mindset. Go back to your "Me Wheel" in Chapter 1. You are more than just one thing, sport, hobby, or endeavor. Remember, failure is feedback—you are never a finished product. Keep growing and learning.

Let's take a closer look at the makeup of a growth mindset.

An individual with a growth mindset:
- Believes skill can grow
- Desires to learn and improve
- Embraces challenges
- Persists in the face of setbacks
- Sees effort as the path to mastery
- Seeks and learns from feedback
- Finds lessons and inspiration in the success of others

There are also several additional distinguishing factors regarding a growth mindset. Individuals with a growth mindset:
- Love a challenge.
- Are resilient.
- Put a deep value in practice.
- Value effort, whereas fixed mindset individuals value image.
- Are able to access a flow state with more frequency than individuals with a fixed mindset.

84

TAKE A MOMENT AND REFLECT ON YOUR MINDSET. ARE YOU OP-
ERATING WITH A FIXED OR GROWTH MINDSET?

Always remember that a way to increase your courage is to
operate with a growth mindset.

Perfection is a Lie

I recently sat down with a student-athlete going off to play
softball in college. She was very stressed about the transition. I asked her two basic questions to get a feel for her
current mindset:

- What do you want?
- What is holding you back?

Her response to the first question was startling, but all too
common with student-athletes. She said, "I want to be perfect."

Her response to the second question came down to her fear
of failure. Fear of getting cut. Fear of losing the opportunity
to play softball. And fear of letting down those around her.

My counsel to her and to you (coming from my own battles
with chasing the unrealistic and unhealthy lie of perfection) is that bearing the weight of perfection will do nothing
but hold you back. When you play "not to fail," you attract
more negative outcomes. Remember to think of your mind
as a filter. Shift your goals and thoughts to be less about
image, opinions, and statistics and more about process
goals that you can control. I call this your ACE: Attitude,
Concentration, and Effort.

In the end, no one can control specific outcomes in competition; however, you can control your ACE. When you op-

timize your internal brain filter to focus on positivity and improvement, anxiety and stress will lessen. When you take away the crippling power from failure, and see it as an opportunity to grow and get better, you will not only increase your likelihood of accessing a flow state, but—more importantly—you will be a happier person, also.

To quote (in my opinion, the greatest rapper of all time) Tupac Shakur, "Trust me, I never lose. I either win or I learn from it." Now that is a winning mindset.

Choose courage over playing it safe. Play big, not small. Be bold. Don't run away from adversity, but attack it. Stretch yourself by operating out of your comfort zone.

Just remember that your missed steps are only failures if you accept defeat. Never surrender, just alter your approach. Don't avoid failure, but seek it out. With this mindset, your skills will improve, and through perseverance, often times your stress level decreases.

Will Smith said it best: "God places the best things in life on the other side of your maximum fear."

WHAT FEAR, PAST FAILURE, NEGATIVE THOUGHT PATTERN, OR ADVERSITY IS HOLDING YOU BACK?

Here's another three-step approach to address what is causing stress in your life:
1. Write it down.

2. Tell someone.
3. Take action.

Just by identifying this fear and writing it down diminishes some of its power. If you are still holding onto a past mistake, write that down, also. Let it live on a page, and not in a loop in your mind. The next step is to talk to someone about it. Finally, even if it is just a small step, take action to address what you have been avoiding.

WHO CAN YOU TALK TO ABOUT YOUR FEAR OR WHAT CAUSES YOU STRESS?

WHAT IS ONE SMALL STEP YOU CAN TAKE TO ATTACK YOUR FEAR? A large part of facing your fear is having a clear picture of what you want. In the next chapter, we will talk about the power of having a clear vision. Vision in how you see yourself and how you see your future.

E + R = O

What do you do when things do not go as planned? Like when you fail or when someone on your team makes a mistake. What do you do when things outside of your control go awry?

To quote Dr. Martin Luther King, Jr., "The ultimate measure of a man is not where he stands in moments of comfort and convenience, but where he stands at times of challenge and controversy."

The definition of one's character (an individual, leader, or team) can be found following an event or outcome—whether good or bad. How do you handle success? Do you get cocky? Do you receive all of your self worth when you win? How about when you lose? When things don't go your way do you practice *BCS—do you Blame, Complain, or Shame others?* The latter approach is an internal and external culture that will never deliver championship results.

Let me share with you to a tool and system introduced to the national powerhouse Ohio State University Football program by leadership consultants Tim and Brian Kight. It's the equation E + R = O. This is a philosophy of taking ownership of your actions regardless of the environment or circumstance.

We can't control the events (E) in our life. Nor can we control the outcomes (O). We do, however, have complete control over our reactions (R).

Here's an example: The beginning of the 2014 season started out like a nightmare for the Ohio State Buckeyes. They finished the previous season with back-to-back losses. To make matters worse, their best player, quarterback Braxton Miller, suffered a season-ending injury during fall camp (Miller won the Big-10 Player of the Year award the previous two seasons). Due to this unthinkable loss, they were forced to start the untested redshirt freshman, J.T. Barrett.

OSU never lost a regular season game in Head Coach Urban Meyer's first two seasons, but this streak ended in the second game of the year. The Buckeyes lost a home game versus Virginia Tech.

This is where the power of E + R = O came into play. The Ohio State program couldn't control or change the event (E) that they lost their best player before the season. They couldn't control that they were forced to start a naive freshman who lacked any experience at all. Also, they couldn't control or change the outcome (O) of their early season loss to Virginia Tech. All they could control was their reaction (R) and response.

Oh, and respond they did! Ohio State rattled off ten consecutive wins including a huge victory over their bitter rival the University of Michigan Wolverines to close out the regular season. The good news: That win earned them a spot in the Big-10 championship game versus Wisconsin. The bad news: Their signal caller, J.T. Barrett, who grew up fast (and even earned first team all-conference honors), suffered a season-ending leg injury. Knowing that they couldn't control the event (E), the Buckeyes had to react (R) in the proper fashion in order to keep their national championship hopes alive. Because of E + R = O, they carried a "next man up" mindset.

Insert third string sophomore quarterback Cardale Jones. In the first start of his career, despite overcoming an early first-half interception (E) Jones led OSU to a 59-0 rout over Wisconsin (R). This win earned the Buckeyes a birth into the first-ever NCAA playoff. The selection committee gave Ohio State a fourth seed aligning them to face the favored one seed Alabama Crimson Tide. Though they couldn't control this event (E) or outcome (O), they took control of their response (R) and not only upset Alabama, but went on to defeat Heisman Trophy winner Marcus Mariota and the Oregon Ducks for a national championship.

In summary, the E + R = O philosophy is this:
1. In life, our character reveals itself by how we react (R) to events (E) that happen to us. For example, you miss a game-winning shot, you get sick, the referee makes a bad call, there's horrible weather, you get injured, or someone on your team makes a mistake. Often times, the event isn't the obstacle, but blaming, complaining, and shaming (BCS) are actions that stand in the way of greatness.
2. Our outcomes (O) are often determined by how we respond to the events that we go through, both positive and negative. This is typically a byproduct of how much time and effort you have invested into your process, habits, and language you speak to yourself and others (is it positive or negative?).
3. You are not defined by whether you win or lose, or whether you fail or succeed (as an individual or team) but how you react.
4. Use failure and adversity as building blocks and learning tools to success, instead of allowing them to be

roadblocks along the path toward your best self.

IS THERE AN EVENT OR OUTCOME IN YOUR PAST THAT YOU ARE LETTING DEFINE YOU? HOW DO YOU RESPOND WHEN THINGS GO BAD DURING YOUR DAY? HOW DO YOU RESPOND TO SUCCESS?

Take ownership of your life and utilize the power of E + R = O.

CHAPTER 4

VISION

THE MOST POWERFUL FORCE IS
HOW YOU SEE YOURSELF

Going into my last football season as a collegiate athlete felt much different than my previous three seasons. Playing baseball was the best thing that could have happened to me. My confidence, perspective, and focus of living in the now greatly improved.

I was finally able to do a better job of quieting the noise. One of the main reasons for this was that I added to my *Me Wheel*. My experience of being a solid contributor to the baseball program allowed me to gain new relationships, stretch my comfort zones, and shift my focus away from football in a healthy way.

My performance improved because my inner-balance improved. Many athletes and performers, however, allow their self-worth and self-love to be tied into their sport or craft. This is a slippery slope. I'm all for setting high standards and holding yourself accountable, but I believe that one of the main reasons why athletes and performers feel stressed is often times a byproduct of balance—or a lack of balance. Their image of who they are is funneled through the lens of their sport.

DO YOU EVER FEEL THAT WAY? IS YOUR SELF-IMAGE DIRECTLY TIED TO YOUR SPORT?

During that initial baseball season, I remember having the internal dialogue in which I would say to myself (especially after failure): I *always have football to fall back on.* Or, *How many other guys out here can juggle two sports?*

I remember hearing a quote that really resonated with me: "When you have nothing to lose, you have everything to gain."

Think about that statement for a second. When you are not overly consumed by outcomes, your muscles are more relaxed, your mind is calmer, and you do not waste any energy worrying about failure. Thus, your performance improves. This mindset usually works when attracting a date, so why not use it in your sport?

Some people believe that they will perform better with a "back against the wall" mentality, or the feeling that they must validate themselves by proving their abilities. The reason why I don't like this mindset is because with this approach, you are giving your power to someone else and allowing someone's opinion to impact your perceived value. Never let another person dictate your self-worth.

The great Greek philosopher, Plato, said it best, "The first and greatest victory is to conquer self." In the end, you are your only competition.

There is a fine balance between caring about your performance while not letting failure define you. I call this approach "Care/Don't Care." As in, *care* about your craft and effort, but *don't care* what others think about you (I know, easier said than done).

Going into my senior summer conditioning program and fall camp, my obsession with failure diminished from a ten to...like a two. If I dropped a pass, the world wasn't going to end. My internal filter was set to neutral or positive—a common place for successful athletes and performers. I was able to limit the amount of negative thoughts that used to plague me, like catastrophizing, seeing only in black and white, or replaying past failures. I found myself worrying less about what I couldn't control.

With this clear vision and self-image, I was able to set a realistic goal for myself. For whatever reason, my freshman, sophomore, and junior football seasons, I didn't set personal statistical goals. Going into my last year, I knew my role, and I had a healthy view of my fit within the offense. We were stacked offensively—especially at the receiver position. My role that season was to be a reliable third or fourth option and to specialize on converting on third downs.

I'll never forget that first game my senior year. We were playing a home game versus the Nevada Wolf Pack in Seattle at CenturyLink Field—the home of the Seahawks. I was excited because Seattle native (O'Dea High School alum and later fourteen-year NFL veteran) Nate Burleson was coming into town. We played together our senior year in the high school East-West All-State game, and I knew that he was primed to have a great year.

The place was packed. More than 60,000 fans were in attendance for this sun-drenched late-August afternoon matchup. We were pre-season favorites to win the conference and everyone within the program could feel the energy and excitement for the season to begin.

Everything began to click for me personally. I created a process that summer and stuck to it—beginning with that first game and continuing through the entire season. I ate the same pre-game meal and listened to the same mix of songs while getting ready in the locker room. I wore the same gear (taped wrists, same socks, spandex, gloves, and shoe style). And I kept my warm-up rituals the same as practice. This consistency helped me limit unnecessary energy in decision-making. It also helped trigger my focus and concentration.

I entered that game with clear and realistic goals:
- Give maximum effort on every play.
- Catch three balls a game.
- Have fun.

On our first drive of the second quarter, I ran a crisp post route from the left side and caught a fifteen-yard gain to help set-up a scoring drive. My second catch came in the third quarter and was a big third-down conversion to get us over mid-field. My third and final catch of the game came again on third down and though we were short, my seven-yard grab over the middle put us into field goal range to add to our fourth quarter lead.

We won the game 31-7, and I walked off the field feeling like I belonged. I hit my game goals on all levels: Quiet mind...check. Play with maximum effort...check. Have fun...double-triple check. And, I hit my catches-per-game goal square on the nose with three catches.

DO YOU SET A CLEAR GAME OBJECTIVE FOR YOURSELF BEFORE YOU COMPETE? IF YOU DON'T, YOU SHOULD. HAVING A CLEAR GOAL GIVES PURPOSE AND HELPS UNLOCK FLOW.

What a difference one year made. My mental and physical performance was a far cry from the season-opener my junior year versus Idaho.

By setting clear objectives for each game that were a bit of a stretch, but attainable, I allowed my subconscious to go to work and execute on my goals. With this mindset, I cracked back into the starting line-up, and as a team, we worked our way up to being ranked third in the country.

In order to be clutch and operate in a flow state, you must have a positive self-image and clear vision (just like I did that season).

Image, Standards, Belief

Take a second to stop what you are doing right now and look up the date and time. Seriously, do this right now. At this very moment, on this very day, you (and your team for that matter) are a byproduct of three things:
1. Your self-image
2. Your standards
3. Your belief

Self-Image

The most powerful force is how you see yourself. When you look in the mirror, or when you think of yourself, what do you see? A victor or victim...winner or whiner...champ or chump...hero or zero...warrior or worrier?

One of the reasons why I love Russell Wilson is not because of his talent, but because of his perspective and belief in his abilities. On paper, there is no way he should be one of the highest paid and most dominant players in the NFL today. After signing a professional baseball contract with the Rockies and playing baseball in the summer of his junior year in college, his football coach at North Carolina State didn't want him back. Thus, Wilson transferred to the University of Wisconsin. After breaking records with his passing efficiency, winning a conference title, and playing in a Rose Bowl, every NFL team passed on this Virginia native multiple times. Many felt that he was too short to be a reliable starter at the professional level.

These setbacks didn't rattle Wilson. After being drafted by the Seattle Seahawks with the seventy-fifth pick overall, Wilson told head coach Pete Carroll, "That was the best decision you ever made."

Wilson's inner-confidence was ingrained in his psyche as a young boy. His father, Benjamin Wilson III (who played both football and baseball at Dartmouth), had a major influence on his son before passing away at the age of fifty-five due to complications with diabetes.

When Wilson was a young teenager, his father told him "Russ, there's a king in every crowd."

The young Wilson then asked his father, "What does that mean?'"

His father explained, "With faith in God, and with help from others, anyone in any crowd can rise to greatness."

This is how I interpret that statement: The only difference between a king (or queen) and a peasant is in the mind. Being undersized and highly doubted doesn't matter.

Wilson has had the mind of the mightiest king his entire career. From winning a Super Bowl and being selected to multiple Pro Bowls, his "Why not me? Why not us?" mantra has served him well. He even established a foundation called "Why Not You?" to empower others with resources and support to change lives for the better. *(For more information on Wilson's foundation, visit whynotyoufdn.org.)*

Wilson sees himself as a champion. He has the self-talk of a champion. He has the habits of a champion. Therefore, he is a champion. Being elite doesn't happen randomly. Being elite is a choice.

SO WHAT DO YOU THINK—ARE TITANS LIKE RUSSELL WILSON BORN OR MADE?

Your self-image sets the stage for what you expect out of yourself, your actions, results, and self-belief.

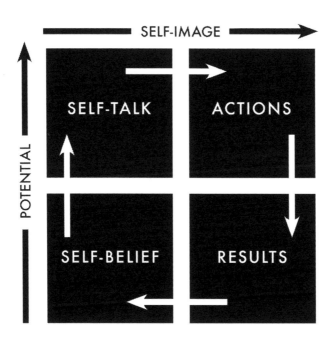

Your self-image also dictates how you let others treat you and what you get out of life. Here's a story to help me explain:

Ayo the Lion
One day in the jungle, a lion, lioness, and their little cub named Ayo were out on a morning walk together. Unfortunately, a gang of hunters spotted them and went in for the kill. To protect his son, the father lion quickly picked up and threw him into the bushes. The lion and lioness sacrificed themselves to save their son. Ayo was safe, but abandoned. He cried and cried because he was scared and ached for his parents.

Luckily though, after a short amount of time, a herd of sheep came by and adopted the lion cub. Ayo grew up with this herd of sheep and even came to believe that he was a sheep. From that point forward, Ayo ate like a sheep, said "bah" like a sheep, followed others like a sheep, and was timid like a sheep.

One day several years later, the new alpha lion and king of the jungle, Desta, was on the outer rim of the jungle and spotted the sheep. He ran after them, but stopped in shock when he saw another lion. All the sheep scattered and fled, including Ayo.

Desta cornered Ayo and said, "What's wrong with you?!" What are you doing with these sheep?"

Ayo replied, "Please have mercy on me, please don't kill me."

Desta couldn't believe what he was seeing. He even asked Ayo to roar, but all Ayo did was bah like a sheep. Disgusted, Desta grabbed Ayo and took him to the nearby river. He told him to look at his reflection in the water. Ayo looked down and saw a beautiful, powerful mane.

He looked back at Desta, then back at the reflection, and back again several times. Desta said, "You are a lion! Now roar like one!"

Ayo puffed out his chest and tried, but all that came out was a weak growl. Desta swiftly slapped Ayo across the face with his powerful paw and said again, "You are a lion! The king of the jungle!—now roar like one!"

Ayo looked back at his reflection and saw his paws and sharp claws; he opened his mouth and saw his enormous teeth. He looked again into the river and a flashback of his brave father came to him. He saw his father in his reflection. And just like that, his self-image changed.

Ayo then stood up and roared the loudest roar the jungle had ever heard. All corners of the jungle could hear this thunderous and powerful sound. Ayo's days as a sheep were over.

HOW DO YOU SEE YOURSELF? DO YOU FOCUS ON YOUR STRENGTHS OR DO YOU GET OVERLY CONSUMED BY YOUR PAST FAILURES AND SHORTCOMINGS?

Another moral of this story is all about who you choose to surrounding yourself with. Successful performance coach Jim Rohn said, "You are a byproduct of the five people you spend the most time with."

Who is in your crew?

Just know that your alignment defines your assignment. Be very careful and selective about who you're spending most of your time with. Are they helping or hurting you be your best self? Their thought processes, words, and habits will rub off on you.

Choose to hang out with lions, not sheep. This means you might need to distance yourself in a polite way with those who are holding you back.

CAN YOU THINK OF ANYONE WHO HAS A NEGATIVE INFLUENCE ON YOU?

ARE YOU A LEADER LIKE A LION? OR A FOLLOWER LIKE A SHEEP?

Strengths
The great philosopher Socrates famously said, "Know thyself." Having a healthy self-image is all about self-awareness.

Because we were stacked with talent at WSU my senior season, I knew if I wanted to get significant playing time that year (and my entire career), I had to look beyond my abilities of running and catching the football. I knew I had to play to my strengths.

Though I lacked dominant size and speed, I was a natural all-around athlete and used my football IQ to my benefit. I was a jack-of-all-trades: I knew all the receiver positions (I could play inside and outside), I was the holder for field goals, the leading punt returner three of my four years, and mostly I was known to Cougar fans as a trick play specialist. Being a former quarterback, I was often used in wide receiver passes. In my college career, I was eleven for

104

twelve, passing for 500 yards and six touchdowns. My only incompletion was on a botched snap on a field goal.

These trick plays were so effective, I later learned that opposing teams would designate
a player on their scout team to mimic me. During practice, they would have a player wear the number 83 (my number) and take their gloves off before a wide receiver pass. Arizona scouted this perfectly and sacked me on a reverse pass.

Before that play, as I lined up on their sidelines with my gloves off, the whole team erupted, "His gloves are off! His gloves are off! Trick play! Trick play!"

It's OK, we still beat them, and I stopped wearing receiver gloves after that.

What Do You Focus on?
Many individuals in sport and in life are overly consumed by their shortcomings. They spend the majority of their time focusing on what they don't have, instead of focusing on what they have (areas in which they are naturally skilled). This is called "playing to your strengths." It's important to continue to improve and learn new skills, but it's equally, if not more important, to enhance areas in which you are naturally strong.

The most successful athletes do this. Tom Brady doesn't try to be Russell Wilson, and Russell Wilson doesn't try to be Tom Brady. Wilson uses his overall athletic ability to create throwing lanes, buy time in the pocket, and run for big gains when he needs to. Brady uses his brain, accurate arm, and excellent pocket presence to shred defenses. Both styles are different but effective.

Albert Einstein broke it down beautifully: "Everybody is a genius. But if you judge a fish by its ability to climb a tree, it will live its whole life believing that it is stupid."

CAN YOU IDENTIFY YOUR BIGGEST STRENGTHS?

HOW CAN YOU BETTER USE YOUR STRENGTHS TO HELP YOUR PER-FORMANCE AND CONTRIBUTION TO YOUR TEAM?

That same game in which I was sacked at Arizona, I cracked my collarbone after a late hit from their safety. This cheap shot forced me out of action for a month. Up until that point, I was right on pace with my goal of three catches per game.

A few individual highlights during that seven-game stretch included earning Chevrolet Player of the Game honors on the road versus sixth-ranked Ohio State University (ESPN GameDay was there), as well as a five-catch performance versus Stanford. I came back at full strength with our regular season-ending game versus UCLA. On the second play of the game, I threw a sixty-six-yard touchdown pass to six-foot-six Mike Bush, which set the tone for our road victory and conference title...and a trip back to the Rose Bowl.

Without a doubt, a healthier self-image helped me perform better. I remember feeling much more excited, grateful, and happier that season. Here's the thing: The happier you are, the better you'll play...period. Playing through rage and anger can only sustain itself for so long.

Feeling good and having a positive internal disposition has been linked to peak performance.

HOW HAPPY ARE YOU RIGHT NOW? WHAT CAN YOU DO IN YOUR LIFE TO GET MORE ENJOYMENT AND CREATE MORE FUN EACH DAY?

Playing to your strengths is more than just doing things in which you are naturally gifted, but it's also what you enjoy doing. Playing to your strengths gives you energy, there's less thinking involved, and it brings deep satisfaction.

Standards

Having a clear vision means being able to identify your standards. Another way to look at standards is to define your core values. Your core values are your guiding principles, internal rules that help you decide what to do and what not to do. When you've clearly defined your standards, you are giving yourself an internal system from which to measure the choices you make.

People who underperform and fall below their potential live with the *illusion of choice.* They give themselves options and let chance take its course. This laissez faire approach hinders sustained peak performance. The Hall of Fame type athletes like Hank Aaron, Usain Bolt, and Billy Jean King know that with clear values, decisions are easy. Excellence doesn't just happen. Excellence is formed by drawing a line in the sand and sacrificing daily for a greater purpose.

Your standards are your moral compass—they guide your behavior. The lower your standards, the lower your level of sustained production.

One of the biggest reasons why we turned around our football program during my tenure at WSU was because we raised the standards of what we expected out of each other as a team. Whether it was our off-season condition-ing program, how we carried ourselves off the field, or our commitment level during the season, we created a culture that expected a high level of effort and accountability. This improved vision of what our standards were made all the difference. (I'll explain this story in more detail in the next chapter.)

Another way to look at standards is to examine your *must do* versus *should do* lists.

Think about your life right now. You have already created an internal set of standards that you *must do*. Whether it is brushing your teeth twice a day (I hope!), getting a cer-tain number of hours of sleep each night, or checking your Snapchat twenty times a day. These non-negotiables with yourself are ingrained into your subconscious, which you will not compromise.

You also have things you *should* do. I *should* drink more water. I *should* do my homework instead of watching Net-flix. I *should* eat less junk food and eat more fruits and veg-etables. I *should* commit more hours to the weight room. I *should* hang out with people who don't abuse drugs and alcohol.

Many people *should* all over themselves. The mind is will-ing, but the flesh is weak. If you want to be a champion, it's time to clearly define your standards and create a system to help hold yourself accountable. I suggest incorporating a teammate or having a mentor to help hold you to your standards.

These standards can be physical and mental. Setting guidelines on your self-talk is just as important as how many repetitions you do on the bench press. It's time to set a higher standard for how you talk to yourself. Fire your inner-critic. Hold yourself to a higher standard with the relationship you have with yourself, as well as your physical effort. Instead of beating yourself up with negative internal words, encourage yourself with affirmations and uplifting internal dialogue. This method will help sustain a higher level of accountability and enjoyment of your craft.

WHAT ARE YOUR STANDARDS? WHAT ARE YOUR NON-NEGO-TIABLES AS A PERFORMER? HOW DO YOU HOLD YOURSELF AC-COUNTABLE? MAKE A LIST OF THESE NOW.

Belief

Living in Seattle, it's pretty awesome to be close to several of the most successful companies in the world, one of which is the e-commerce juggernaut, Amazon.com. My wife, Kendra, worked as a graphic designer for Amazon for four years. The company's growth has been staggering. In the third quarter of 2017, Amazon posted $43.7 billion in net sales, and CEO Jeff Bezos surpassed his Seattle billionaire buddy, Microsoft founder Bill Gates, as the richest person in the world. But, did you know that Amazon didn't make a profit until the fifth year of operation? Bezos' vision, belief, and commitment to his goals kept his pioneering company on a specific path. This discipline and clarity helped Amazon survive the dot-com bubble burst of the early 2000s.

Bezos said, "We're stubborn on vision and flexible on details." Through Bezos' leadership, Amazon is unwavering on its destination, but adaptable on how to get there. Bezos' vision is shaping how we live today and the future that we will live in tomorrow.

Bezos got started because he had a goal. In 1994, Bezos

saw a statistic that people utilizing the World Wide Web was growing 2,300 percent each month. He felt inspired and decided to get out of his Wall Street investment career. He borrowed his parents' life savings and began selling books out of his garage through the Internet.

Bezos' belief in and expectations of himself, as well as those around him, helped his company achieve goals that most people couldn't even see. Amazon continues to evolve and tap into new markets. It recently acquired Whole Foods for $14 billion as part of Bezos' long-term diversification strategy. Many investing experts were puzzled by this acquisition, but Bezos is staying true to his vision, goals, and belief.

Goals help give your subconscious a roadmap and the GPS coordinates to where you want to go. Though having a vision of what you want is important, the more powerful question is: *How can you become what you don't believe?*

While studying and learning from top performers in a variety of fields (athletics, sales, leadership, school), I've found that self-belief is at the foundation of their successes. Having faith in yourself and something bigger than you are prerequisites for sustained peak performance. To copy one of the most successful advertising campaigns ever ("Got Milk?"), I ask, **"Got Belief?"**

Improved Image Creates Improved Actions
This concept of belief is seeing is trusting something that hasn't happened yet.

Before Geno Auriemma was hired as the head women's basketball coach at the University of Connecticut in 1985, the Huskies had only one winning season in the program's history. Auriemma turned that around quickly. After going 13-15 in his first season, UCONN has posted more than

110

thirty consecutive winning seasons, including eleven national titles (an unmatched feat).

Like any successful athlete, coach, CEO, or leader, you must not only be able to see where you want to go, but you have to believe you can get there, also. With a positive sense of self and clear vision, your actions will follow your image.

Auriemma—also a two-time Olympic gold medal winning coach—said, "It's about doing it in a way that it can't be done any better. That is the goal every day."

Auriemma's vision helped him hire a skilled staff, recruit the right talent, and create a culture of excellence. Coach Auriemma's belief and standards raised the level of play and production of those around him and is why he is arguably the greatest basketball coach of all time—in men's or women's hoops.

Raising your belief-system to achieve your goals doesn't just relate to athletics.

Why did Grammy award-winning rapper Drake hustle so hard after blazing onto the hip hop scene is 2009? Because he had a goal and an unwavering belief in himself. He wanted to amass $25 million in earnings by the age of twenty-five. Once he accomplished that vision, he raised his goal to $250 million before the age of thirty. His expectations raised his commitments. His commitments increased his production. His production earned him awards, accolades, credibility, and more than enough money.

Just like Bezos, Auriemma's UCONN Huskies, and Drake demonstrated, if you can see where you want to go before it happens, believe you have what it takes to get there, and put in the work—nothing will stop you from reaching your vision.

Goals

When you mix goals with belief, you give your subconscious a clear purpose. For example, the jumping off point for our string of successes as a football program was the fact that we broke every workout with one common chant: "Pac-10 champs." We said this collectively over and over again. We raised our expectations as a unit, and our program raised its level of accountability, which improved our production. The combination of standards, belief, and goals is powerful.

DO YOU HAVE A GOAL? HAVE YOU WRITTEN IT DOWN? DO YOU HAVE A PLAN TO ACHIEVE IT?

In the book, *What They Don't Teach You at Harvard Business School,* author Mark McCormack shares a study about the students in the 1979 MBA program. The students were asked these three questions:
1. Do you have a goal?
2. Have you written it down?
3. Do you have a plan to achieve it?

The results were astonishing: 84 percent had no specific goals or plans; 13 percent had some idea of a goal but did not write it down with a plan; and only 3 percent of the students had written down their goals and had plans to achieve them.

Ten years later, the graduates were interviewed again. What the researchers found was amazing. The 3 percent who had written down their goals and plans were earning an average of ten times more money than the other 97 percent combined. That's like making $50,000 per year versus

$500,000! What sounds better to you? It's time you write down your goals and action plans.

WRITE DOWN YOUR GOALS IN THE THREE DIFFERENT TIME FRAMES BELOW:
- THIS SEASON
- ONE YEAR
- THREE TO FIVE YEARS

In the next chapter, we will talk about creating an action plan for these goals.

Philosophy
For the first time in his football coaching career, Pete Carroll was out of a job. After getting fired from two stops as a head coach in the NFL (first with the New York Jets, then the New England Patriots), Carroll had extra time on his hands to reflect. It was gut-check time. He knew he wanted to stay in coaching, but on his terms. Inspired by UCLA legendary basketball coach John Wooden, Carroll decided to write down his coaching philosophy—something that had a huge impact for Wooden. After not winning an NCAA national title until sixteen seasons at UCLA, the "Wizard of Westwood" (Wooden) clearly identified his philosophy, which he called the "Pyramid of Success." With this clear vision, he went on to win ten national titles in twelve years.

After his firing from the Patriots, and motivated by Wooden's books, Carroll brought his "If you want to win forever, always compete" mantra to his interview with then-University of Southern California Athletic Director Mike Garrett. This clarity of vision paid off. Carroll and the Trojans dominated the 2000s with their performance, winning multiple conference titles and national championships. When many critics said that rah-rah style wouldn't work at the professional level, Carroll didn't waver with his approach. He took the same philosophy to the Seattle Seahawks and shook up the NFL. This mindset and leadership earned Carroll and the 'Hawks multiple division titles and trips to the Super Bowl.

If it worked for Wooden and Caroll, why not put this exercise to use for yourself?

Carroll suggests you keep your personal philosophy simple and under twenty-five words.

To help with this, let me offer you a system to guide you in defining your philosophy:

Having a clear vision and philosophy is all about defining your **MVPs**. The MVP (Most Valuable Player) is awarded to the best player of a given team or league. In order to be the best version of you, it's time that you define your MVPs:

- *Mission* (What is your vision statement for the future— what do you want to be known for?)
- *Values* (What are three to five guiding principles that will guide your behavior?)
- *Purpose* (What is the "why" behind your goal?)
- *Slogan* (Can you come up with a slogan or hashtag that will help drive action—e.g., "ALWAYS COMPETE?")

Virtually all successful organizations like Amazon and the Seahawks can identify their MVPs (or some other system). Clarity is power. Decide what your MVPs are and improve your vision. Let this serve as your guide not only to being the best athlete you can be, but being the best person you can be, also.

WRITE DOWN YOUR VISION IN THESE FOUR AREAS:

- M - MISSION
- V - VALUES
- P - PURPOSE
- S - SLOGAN

Once you've completed this crucial step in developing your vision, the next step is to identify key actions needed to help you get to where you want to go. In Chapter 5, we will talk about the importance of taking control of your effort and habits. I'll also help you create a solid plan to achieve your goals.

ATTACK FEAR

Fear kills more dreams than failure ever will.

What do you fear?

Is it failure? Are you overly consumed by your image and what people think of you? Or is it a past mistake that you keep replaying over and over? Or maybe you suffer from one of the most crippling fears, which used to often plague me—negative anticipation. You worry about events that haven't even happened yet. You use phrases like "don't let this happen," or "avoid this."

The following statement sums up this negative thought pattern: "**What you resist, persists.**"

Fear feeds off of fear. The more you avoid, the more you attract. Whether you think positive or negative thoughts, often times you also attract positive or negative outcomes in your life. When you create pictures of what you "don't want," you are creating that image in your mind, and thus attracting that very event.

Have you ever played baseball and been on defense and thought, "Don't hit it to me, don't hit it to me." What happens? The ball always finds you.

Or you didn't do your homework for school. You show up to class and you keep saying to yourself, *Don't call on me, don't call on me.* What happens? Without a doubt, the teacher calls on you.

An amazing story of the power of thought and fear comes from Puyallup High School (Washington state) class of 2017 standout quarterback, Nathaniel Holcomb. As a sophomore, Holcomb earned the varsity starting quarterback position for the Vikings. Like many first-time performers, the desire not to fail consumed Holcomb's mind more than thoughts of making positive things happen.

"I didn't want to screw up," he said. "I didn't want to throw an interception. I was afraid of what people thought of me—even if I didn't know them."

This internal dialogue sounds very familiar to me, as well as many athletes I work with. Ironically, this "don't screw up" mindset leads to more screwing up. One of the biggest mental hurdles for Holcomb that season was the fear of injury.

"I played timid and hesitant," he said. "I was afraid of getting hurt."

Playing to avoid injury instead of playing to make things happen proved detrimental. In week four that season, Holcomb suffered a concussion that kept him out for most of the season.

Entering his junior season, Holcomb grew stronger and more confident. He was more comfortable with the offense, and he knew his playbook. His production improved early in the season, which was evident when he led a come-from-

118

behind victory over Curtis High School. After amassing over one thousand yards passing and eleven touchdowns, however, Holcomb's negative mindset crept back in.

"I remember thinking, *You're doing good, just don't get hurt,*" Holcomb said.

Then, during a mid-season game, his fear of injury manifested itself again. After throwing two touchdowns, a hard hit to his left knee forced a sprained MCL. Holcomb was once again out for the season.

According to performance psychologist Heidi Grant from Columbia University, "The brain can process five to seven different thoughts at a time. But when the brain is anxious, it can only process two or three."

This function may be for our evolutionary survival (when avoiding lions and tigers, it's probably important to have a narrow focus). When needing to process a great deal of information at once (like playing quarterback), a relaxed and calm mindset is much more beneficial.

Going into his senior season, Holcomb knew he wanted to make that year different. He committed himself to train even harder, and more importantly, spend less time worrying about things out of his control—like being consumed by other people's opinions and the fear of injury.

"The word 'injury' was not in my mind," Holcomb said. "*My mindset shifted from don't get hurt, to 'I'm going to stay healthy and have a good year.*"

"I said to myself, *I'm not afraid of throwing an interception.*"

A healthy internal dialogue makes all the difference.

I had the pleasure of delivering several mindset workshops with the Puyallup High School football team that summer. One of the messages I gave was on the concept of attacking fear. I encouraged the players not to run away from adversity and challenge, but to attack it head-on. True champions have the courage to face their fears and use that force as powerful energy.

Why did Bruce Wayne (Batman) choose a nocturnal flying creature as his alter ego and symbol of justice? Because of his fear of bats as a young boy. By embracing that fear, and facing it, it gave him courage and strength.

When speaking with the PHS football team, I challenged the seniors to come up with a slogan and a hashtag for the season to serve as their mantra and battle cry. This word or phrase would spark vision and action. Holcomb decided to embrace the mantra "ATTACK FEAR."

"I never heard those two words together—'attack fear,'" Holcomb said. "I liked it and wanted to use it."

Oh, and attack fear he did. When week four came again his senior season, Holcomb didn't get hurt, he hurt the opposing team and dominated. Against South Kitsap High School, Holcomb set a Washington State eleven-man football record with ten touchdown passes—after overcoming two early interceptions.

"I wasn't scared," he said. "I was smarter and more loose in the pocket. I was able to avoid defenders and make more plays."

By attacking his fear, Holcomb went on to finish the season with a clean bill of health. He torched the South Puget Sound League, finishing the year with forty-two touchdowns, only nine interceptions, and 3,649 yards passing.

This performance earned him several post-season honors and a spot with the College of Idaho in the Frontier League. We can learn from Holcomb's story. By facing fear, adversity, and challenge head-on, we take away its power, and in turn, become more powerful.

Like Holcomb learned, when faced with FEAR, we have two options:

Forget
Everything
And
Run

or

Face
Everything
And
Rise

The choice is yours.

WHAT FEAR ARE YOU GOING TO ATTACK TODAY?

Use Holcomb's story to inspire you. You got this. Let's go!

CHAPTER 5

EARN IT

WHAT YOU DO IN THE DARK
SHINES BRIGHT IN THE LIGHT

During my time as a WSU football player, I was part of a level of success on the Palouse that had never happened before and has not happened since. During that historic run, we had three consecutive ten-win seasons, went to three bowl games in a row—including a Sun Bowl victory over Purdue, won a conference championship and trip to the Rose Bowl (we lost to Oklahoma), and achieved a Holiday Bowl victory over fifth ranked Texas (whose quarterback Vince Young later won the Heisman Trophy). That was the first time the Cougs had ever advanced to back-to-back bowl games, let alone three in a row.

Going from seven bowl games in seventy-five years to three bowl games in three consecutive years was quite a drastic improvement. Honestly though, we weren't that bad the year before our Sun Bowl season. We actually should have gone to a bowl game. Though we had four wins on the season, we lost three games in overtime and got beat in the final seconds in two other games. We had the talent to be a winning team, but we did not do the little things that successful teams do. We lacked the commitment, synergy, and ability to finish close games.

If I can pinpoint one common denominator that changed everything and propelled our winning ways, it was the fact that we changed our culture—and it all started with peer leadership. The summer before our first ten-win season, all scholarship players and several walk-ons stayed on campus over the summer to train together.

Some of the leaders on the team, myself included, noticed that several players were not showing up to workouts, and if they were there, they were not giving maximum effort. Luckily for us, we had one of the greatest leaders in WSU's history who was determined to change this.

Imagine never losing a game in your life. Well, that was our quarterback, all-league and conference player of the year, Jason Gesser. As the quarterback at the perennial powerhouse Saint Louis High School in Honolulu, Hawaii, Gesser never lost a game as a high school starter. Winning was in his DNA, and he brought that pedigree and expectation to Pullman. Gesser left the Cougar program as the all-time leader in many categories—including the one of most importance, most wins—but his first year as a starter didn't settle well with him. A record of 4-7 was not going to cut it.

I remember a moment after a loss versus Stanford at home, Gesser was furious. After getting beat during that home opener, our six-foot-one 200-pound leader, who spoke with a Hawaiian Pidgin accent, was screaming at the top of his lungs inside the tunnel by our locker room.

"I don't lose! Aaaah! I...never...lose!"

While he was letting out his frustration, he had to stop mid-yell because he had badly bruised ribs. While Gesser was hunched over in pain, I helped him up and into the locker room.

Fast-forward nine months: I saw that same fire on this dry, hot June day in Pullman. That summer we identified a problem. The old way of lifting weights as a team wasn't working. Each player would show up to the weight room and receive a workout card with no supervision. The expectation was to perform your workout, fill out your card, and turn it in when you were done. Many players abused this system and were not doing all their lifts, but would simply fill out their card and turn it in.

Luckily, we had a new strength and conditioning coach that year, Rob Oviatt. Coach "O" (as we called him) came from big-time SEC programs like Louisiana State University and University of Kentucky. He helped increase our accountability and unity. Once he took over, instead of being on our own to lift, we attacked each station in groups. A unit couldn't move on to the next lift until everyone finished. Coach O increased our level of intensity, but there were still players who lacked commitment.

After two weeks of being on campus for summer conditioning, a few of us leaders got together because some guys were not showing up to our morning lifting sessions...or some guys would show up, but be late...or some of the guys who showed up did not take it seriously.

In college athletics, coaches are not allowed to coach on the practice field during the off-season except during specified periods of the year. That is why during these summer months, we had to coordinate and run our own practices and drills. Those first two weeks, we did not get full attendance or effort.

Gesser was fed up.

"This has to stop," he said, after a morning workout "We need to have a players-only meeting. The days of guys not showing up and giving it their all are over. Either you're in or you're out."

125

Hard-hitting safety, senior captain, Billy Newman, joined in: "If we want to turn this program around, we have to have everybody all-in."

The word got out: Players-only meeting in the south stands of Martin Stadium that night, at 5 p.m.

Before our practice started, everyone gathered together. Gesser, Newman, and some other leaders, including me, set the expectation that if you wanted to be a part of this team, you had to be 100 percent committed.

No more being late. No more laziness. No more being selfish.

We made it real simple: If you want to be a Cougar, wear the Crimson and Gray on Saturdays with your brothers, and build a championship team, you have to show up each day with full focus and effort during practices. To illustrate this, we got up, walked down the bleachers, and crossed the line in the end zone.

This was the challenge: "Cross this line and commit. Or don't cross this line and quit."

We said, "Once you step over this line, you are committing to yourself, your teammates, and this program. If you don't agree to be all-in, we don't want you on this team."

Wow, what a powerful exercise. Everyone there that night crossed the line. From that point on, we were a different team. Multiple units, but one heart beat. We even broke every workout together as a team with the same chant, "Pac-10 champs!"

The tone was set. The vision was created. And the expectation for our level of commitment was established. The rest

126

is history.

Here's the thing about flow—the more you practice and put in the hours to improve yourself (especially in a group with a common goal), the easier it is to unlock its power. This chapter is all about understanding that in order to excel in any endeavor, whether in sport, medicine, art, business, or life in general, you have to commit to winning habits. You have to put in the work. In other words, *you have to earn it.*

When you've put in the thousands of hours necessary to be a champion, you build credibility with your own internal dialogue. Your subconscious goes to work. Your stress level goes down. You trust your instincts and preparation, and your performance improves. Kind of like when Golden State Warriors' Kevin Durant nailed the game-winning three-pointer in game three of the 2017 NBA Finals.

After this clutch bucket versus LeBron James and the Cleveland Cavaliers, a reporter challenged Durant's shot selection. In a post-game interview on the court, she asked something like, "Down two points, with forty seconds left, why did you take that transition three-point shot?"

The MVP and world champion replied with (and I'm paraphrasing here): "I trusted what I saw. LeBron was behind the line and back-pedaling. I've practiced and made that shot thousands of times. I didn't even think. I had to take it."

Boom. By putting in the work, Durant's inner-game let his body take over, and splash!—he nailed the biggest shot of his life, and the Warriors went on to win their second title in three years.

The art of being clutch is developed over time. It doesn't just show up. Like our WSU football team and Durant demonstrated, we don't rise to the occasion, we rise to our training (and commitment to prepare the right way).

Think about trees in a storm. The trees that survive the storm have established roots underground for many many years. The trees with shallow roots undoubtedly get damaged and knocked down. Trees can't grow roots overnight.

As performers, we are not much different. The storm is coming eventually, so what are you doing to grow your roots?

Time
Do you know how many hours are in a week?

The answer is 168. What are you doing with your time? If you take away roughly eight hours per night for sleep, and eight hours of work or school per day, that adds up to one hundred hours. This means you have sixty-eight hours left. The most successful people are able to do more with their 168.

WHAT ARE YOU DOING WITH YOUR 168?

Successful author Malcolm Gladwell has a theory. He believes that in order to be an expert and achieve mastery in any field, you must put in 10,000 hours of practice (this concept is from the his national bestselling book *Outliers*). He references The Beatles (who performed all-night shows in Hamburg before making it big) and Bill Gates (who worked on computers since his teen years) among other examples. Whether you believe this to be true or not (many researchers challenge this claim), one thing is certain: There is no such thing as an overnight success.

128

University of Pennsylvania psychologist Angela Duckworth describes this fortitude as "having grit." According to Duckworth, grit is made up of two elements: passion and perseverance. Passion is defined as the consistency of one's interest over very long periods of time—years, decades or even a lifetime. Perseverance relates to the tenacity with which one approaches goals—the ability to carry on through times of frustration, boredom, hardship, and pain.

Pop music icon Justin Bieber began playing the drums at age three. Taylor Swift took guitar lessons and began to write music at age eleven. Peyton Manning's sixteen- to eighteen-hour workdays preparing for games on Sunday were legendary. The reality is, in order to be great and master a skill, you must put in the time, as in years of refining and practicing your skills (like Bieber and Swift) and enough hours before it's time to perform (like Manning). What the greats like Bieber, Swift, and Manning also have is the ability to withstand a plethora of adversities and setbacks.

Bieber was a Canadian import who lacked a consistent influence from his father. Swift was an awkward teenager who got picked on at school. Manning overcame a seemingly career-ending neck injury to break records and then solidified his legacy by winning a second Super Bowl.

Not only do you need to put in the time, but you need to have the inner-drive to fight through rejection, setbacks, and feeling uncomfortable. These traits are a prerequisite for greatness.

Obstacles are inevitable. Grit is optional.

A way to help overcome adversities and give yourself stamina to continue for the long haul is to clearly define *why* you play and *why* you want to achieve your goals.

Just make sure that your *why* (or purpose) is for you (internal motivation) versus because you feel pressure from someone else (external motivation).

TAKE A MOMENT AND WRITE DOWN THE REASONS **WHY** YOU PLAY YOUR SPORT OR PERFORM.

NOW WRITE DOWN **WHY** YOU WANT TO ACHIEVE YOUR GOALS.

This exercise will hopefully help give you the grit needed to keep pushing when things get hard. Having a clear purpose is a powerful performance enhancer.

Sacrifice
We live in an era of Netflix, Twitter, and Amazon Prime. Many are obsessed with instant gratification. People become famous almost overnight with YouTube and social media. While researching elite performers and reflecting on my career, however, there is a common theme that deals with greatness, and that is *sacrifice*. To be a champion, you can't be like everyone else. This might sound overly simplistic, but to be uncommon, you must break the mold. Because in the end, winners do what others are not willing to do.

One of my best friends, Charly Martin (author of the *Master Your Mindset* foreword), who set Division II records as a wide receiver and played for five seasons in the NFL, has not had one sip of soda pop since sixth grade. He had a goal to be a professional football player and was willing to make the necessary sacrifices with his training, eating habits, and the choices he made off the field in order to achieve

130

his goals.

WHAT SACRIFICES ARE YOU MAKING TO BE A CHAMPION?

Penn State Head Football Coach James Franklin knows the importance of sacrifice. Being the son of a single mom who was the janitor at his high school, he learned at an early age that nothing significant comes without a significant work ethic. While traveling around the country at various stops during his coaching career (including Washington State University and Vanderbilt), Franklin established five core values that he expects out of his staff, his players, and himself. He shared these values while giving a TEDx Talk on the campus of Penn State University:
1. Relationships
2. Positive attitude
3. Compete
4. Work ethic
5. Sacrifice

At this TEDx Talk, Franklin asked the group, "Are you willing to sacrifice things that the common man won't sacrifice to be special?" He added, "Everybody wants success, but are you willing to sacrifice to do the things you have to do to be successful long-term?"

Some athletes, like former NFL number one overall draft pick quarterback JaMarcus Russell, lose sight of the power of sacrifice. After dominating at Louisiana State University, winning all-conference honors and the 2007 Sugar Bowl, the six-foot-six 260-pound Russell was one of the most exciting prospects since Drew Bledsoe. He had all of the tools and physical abilities to be worthy of the number one pick, which is why the Oakland Raiders chose Russell.

After missing all of training camp during his rookie season due to contract negotiations, Russell didn't make his first start until the last game of that 2007 season. He showed up the next season overweight and his play didn't improve. The following season, the Raiders brought in several other quarterbacks, because from some reports, Russell's weight neared three hundred pounds. His lack of production (twenty-three interceptions, fifteen lost fumbles, and a league-low 50.0 passer rating in 2009), forced the Raiders to cut this once promising prospect. After several unsuccessful comeback attempts, Russell will go down in history as one of the biggest busts in NFL history. So much talent and ability, but no commitment and sacrifice.

At WSU, we had a sign put in our weight room to remind us of the importance of sacrifice. Our strength coach wanted to remind us, "There are two pains in life: pain of regret and pain of hard work."

Trust me, the pain of regret hurts far worse.

NFL coaching legend Vince Lambarti once said, "The man on top of the mountain didn't fall there."

Like these examples show, if you want to be on top of the mountain in whatever it is in life that you want to do, you must put in the time and do what positive psychologists like Dr. Angela Duckworth call "deliberate practice."

TAKE A MOMENT AND REFLECT ON YOUR PRACTICE HABITS. ARE YOU GIVING EVERYTHING YOU HAVE TO IMPROVE YOUR GAME?

Deliberate Practice
In the field of performance psychology, there is a general

132

consensus that in order to develop a level of mastery in a specific field (chess, music, athletics), one must practice— and when I say practice, I mean practice a lot. But it's not just practicing that counts. It's how you practice. The most skilled practitioners in any given field practice with what I call the "Three Gs of Greatness: Goals, Grit, and Growth":

1. **Goals** – *They practice with a specific objective and purpose.*
> » For example, while growing up in Blaine, Washington, basketball prodigy Luke Ridnour often found all of the basketball hoops occupied at open gym. Instead of competing for open hoops to take shots, Ridnour set a goal to improve his ball handling skills. He would spend hours putting himself through various intense dribbling drills. This mastery paid off. Luke was selected as a McDonald's High School All-American, awarded Pac-12 Player of the Year as a junior at the University of Oregon, and had a solid twelve-year career in the NBA.

2. **Grit** – *They practice consistently with passion and perseverance. They are able to overcome obstacles and setbacks because of their determination and commitment.*
> » For example, Dallas Cowboys Hall of Fame receiver Michael Irvin would intentionally make practice harder than games. In the one hundred-degree Texas heat, he would wear sweats and a heavy sweatshirt to weigh himself down. This technique made running and catching the football more challenging than on game day. This practice helped earn Irvin several Super Bowl championships and trips to the Pro Bowl.

3. **Growth** – *They see failure as feedback and an opportunity to improve. They are constantly searching for ways to get better.*

133

» For example, two-time Super Bowl Champion line-backer Ray Lewis said practice time was where he would try new things and get creative with his play. This experimentation, he said, allowed him to learn from failure, which helped him execute at a higher level during games.

This *Three Gs of Greatness* concept can best be described as "deliberate practice," and it's incredibly powerful.

In the scholarly paper, *The Role of Deliberate Practice in the Acquisition of Expert Performance,* Florida State University psychologist and scientific researcher, K. Anders Ericsson, said: "We agree that expert performance is qualitatively different from normal performance and even that expert performers have characteristics and abilities that are qualitatively different from or at least outside the range of those of normal adults. However, we deny that these differences are immutable, that is, due to innate talent. Only a few exceptions, most notably height, are genetically prescribed. Instead, we argue that the differences between expert performers and normal adults reflect a life-long period of deliberate effort to improve performance in a specific domain."

Basically, what Ericsson said (without all the big words), is that it's not about what you're born with, it's about how consistently and deliberately you work on your skills to improve the talent that you have.

Talent is given. Skill is earned. A high level of mastery is developed only through hours of intense, deliberate practice aimed at achieving a specific goal. For example, instead of just showing up to take batting practice, select one area you'd like to work on to improve. Focus on that skill with a clear intention. Ericsson found this approach was a key predictor of peak performance (in music, sport, and many other fields).

134

I'll take skill over talent every day of the week.

Individuals who master a skill do not have to be people with freakish natural abilities. My college baseball teammate Jay Miller is a prime example. Miller is maybe five-foot-nine and weighed about 175 pounds during his playing days. Yet, with a relentless commitment to hitting and working on his timing, he left WSU as the all-time leader in hits. No one took more batting practice with what we called "Iron Mike" (our mechanical pitching machine) than Miller. He could be found on nights, weekdays, and weekends hammering away on Iron Mike. This commitment paid off. He surpassed the career hit totals of MLB standouts like John Olerud, Ron Cey, and Scott Hatteberg.

The elite, like Miller (who was later drafted by the Philadelphia Phillies), are experts at maintaining high levels of practice through setting specific goals and taking on new challenges in order to improve their performance. These high-performing individuals are also open to receive feedback in order to keep refining their skills.

In the Facebook Watch documentary film, *Tom vs. Time,* arguably the greatest football player to ever grace the gridiron, Tom Brady, was shown taking feedback from a throwing specialist during the 2017 off-season. Even though Brady was turning forty years old and had won five Super Bowls up to that point, he was still intentionally looking to improve his game and receive the necessary coaching to get better. If the GOAT (Greatest of All Time) is open to coaching and feedback, it's fair to say that if you want to be exceptional, you should be open to constructive criticism as well.

HOW DO YOU RECEIVE FEEDBACK? ARE YOU OPEN TO COACH-
ING OR DO YOU DEFLECT, MAKE EXCUSES, OR BECOME DEFEN-
SIVE WHEN YOU RECEIVE CONSTRUCTIVE TIPS TO IMPROVE YOUR
GAME?

How Do You Practice?

Let's take the game of tennis, for example. Pretend you
and a friend are learning to play tennis for the first time.
During the first hour session, you learn how to hold the
racquet, have the right stance, and how to swing properly.
You spend the majority of that session hitting the ball off a
wall in front of you.

After that session, you've improved and become comfortable enough to begin to hit the ball over the net from a
machine. The thought of hitting the ball off the wall for
another hour seems boring anyway.

After that hour session with the machine, you respond fa-
vorably to the feedback from your coach, and begin to vol-
ley with another person and really enjoy taking on that new
challenge. After three hours of lessons, you notice your
skills have drastically improved and you are eager to continue your training.

Your friend's experience, however, is much different. His
three sessions consist of simply hitting the ball off the wall
the entire time. He is unsure of his ability to face the tennis ball machine, let alone another person, and he is insecure about receiving feedback. Though he puts in the same
amount of time and energy as you, his skills didn't improve
as much as yours.

This example illustrates the importance of not just practicing to practice, but of making practice like a game: Have

goals, challenge your abilities, seek constructive feedback, and learn from failure.

HAVE YOU EVER BEEN AFRAID TO TAKE THE NEXT STEP AND CHAL-LENGE YOURSELF IN YOUR SPORT OR OTHER AREAS OF YOUR LIFE?

Many people prefer to stay on the first level, or in a lower division, or they tell themselves they can't take the next step.

It's too hard.

I might fail.

What will others think?

What would they say about me?

Do you think those thoughts ever stopped Ichiro Suzuki, Elon Musk, or Danica Patrick from dominating? Definitely not.

Grammer's Grit
Here's one of my favorite stories on the importance of deliberate practice:

Multi-platinum recording artist Andy Grammer did not start out on the top of the charts. In fact, he started out as a street performer in Santa Monica on the Third Street Promenade. To pay bills and make a living, this Los Angeles native and California State University Northridge graduate played for strangers hoping to get tips. He learned early that his original work wasn't getting noticed.

However, when he played catchy, well-known songs like Maroon 5's "Sunday Morning," he would gather a larger crowd. After months and even years of improving his craft and writing hundreds of songs, Grammer finally honed in on his own unique sound that random strangers enjoyed. He then started to garner larger crowds and more tips. This was a result of his hours upon hours of practicing, getting audience feedback, and perfecting his skills.

Though these conditions were necessary for Grammer's growth, they did not generate an ideal lifestyle. Hustling on the street created a great deal of stress and days of wondering if he would have enough money to pay the rent. His relentlessness, passion, and talent finally caught the attention of a record company, though, and he signed his first contract. But just signing a deal doesn't mean you're going to make it. It took two albums and writing more than one hundred songs before Grammer released his breakout hit, "Honey I'm Good," which was a top-ten hit and received radio play all around the world.

The moral of the story: Have passion, patience, and practice your butt off. When you do that, good things will come.

TAKE A MOMENT AND LIST AT LEAST FIVE ACTION STEPS YOU MUST TAKE IN ORDER TO ACHIEVE YOUR GOAL. MAKE SURE YOU ADD A FREQUENCY, TIME, OR DATE NEXT TO THAT ACTION. THIS WILL HELP YOU BETTER MEASURE AND HOLD YOURSELF ACCOUNTABLE.

Commitments
If the commitment doesn't match the dream, there is no dream.

While working with a top-ranked high school baseball team on mental performance, I led an exercise to help them get ready for the post-season. I first asked everyone on the team, including coaches, to write on a piece of paper their goal for the sixteen-team state tournament. After everyone finished, I had several of the players and coaches share their goal.

A pattern emerged: Everyone said their goal was to win the state championship.

I thanked them for sharing, then asked, "How many other teams in this tournament have the same goal of being state champions?"

Several players replied, "Probably all of them."

"Exactly," I said.

I let them know that goals are great, but we can't always control when and if they'll come true. What we can control is what we commit to do to get there.

I gave everyone a new piece of paper. Instead of having them write down a new goal, I had them write down one commitment they pledged to do to help their team win. It was pretty awesome to see what the guys came up with. Each commitment was more about effort, attitude, and a level of focus—all of which they could control.

I had a banner made with their team slogan on it and had everyone write down their one commitment and sign their name on that banner. The team put this banner in their dugout throughout the tournament for inspiration and a friendly reminder to focus on their one commitment. With this shift of attention away from outcomes and toward

139

something more controllable (like one's commitment), they were able to transfer that powerful exercise and win the state title.

Pretty awesome, right?

TAKE A MOMENT AND WRITE DOWN WHAT YOU WILL COMMIT TO DO TO MAKE YOUR GOAL A REALITY.

Habits

An impactful way to improve your performance is to select a commitment and turn it into a habit. The *Merriam-Webster Online Dictionary* defines "habit" as:

noun

A behavior pattern acquired by frequent repetition or physiologic exposure that shows itself in regularity or increased facility of performance; an acquired mode of behavior that has become nearly or completely involuntary.

We are what we repeatedly do. Repetition is the mother of mastery. Our successes and failures are often times a by-product of our habits, which are formed on a subconscious level.

CAN YOU THINK OF A HABIT YOU CURRENTLY HAVE THAT HINDERS YOUR PERFORMANCE?

Jacksonville Jaguars running back Fred Taylor was coming up on a contract year. He was plagued by injuries his previous few seasons, and he knew he had to play his best in order to not only earn a lucrative new contract, but also extend his career. Taylor needed a new plan and was looking to break the nickname of "Fragile Fred."

To help with this, Jackson sought help from mental performance coaches within the organization, Chad Bohling (now the director of mental conditioning with the New York Yankees, who also consults with the Dallas Cowboys) and Trevor Moawad. Researching what other players did within the Jacksonville organization to stay healthy, Bohling and Moawad uncovered a common habit that these individuals performed daily. They simply told Taylor to show up to to the practice facility two hours early. That's it.

Taylor was never late, but he would arrive only five to ten minutes before their morning meetings. By making this one habit shift, and arriving two hours early, it created a cascade of other positive habits. He was able to keep a consistent routine, eat a healthy breakfast, get more treatment in the training room, get extra lifting and conditioning in if needed, and spend more time in the film room.

This one habit change made all the difference. Not only did Taylor stay healthy, but he had one of the most productive seasons in franchise history. His performance earned him a trip to the Pro Bowl, as well as a hefty new contract.

The power of habit is real. This example of isolating one key habit is what author Charles Duhigg calls a "keystone habit" in his book *The Power of Habit*. A keystone habit sets off a chain reaction for other good habits to follow.

LIKE TAYLOR'S EXAMPLE, WHAT IS ONE KEYSTONE HABIT THAT YOU COMMIT TO DO (THAT TRUMPS ALL OTHERS) TO IMPROVE YOUR PERFORMANCE?

Earn It

I love the following statement from (in my opinion) one of the greatest presidents of all time, Abraham Lincoln. When asked how he would chop down a tree, he said, "Give me six hours to chop down a tree, and I will spend the first four sharpening the axe."

The highest achievers are elite because of an elite level of preparation.

While working on mental conditioning with a Major League Baseball player during his off-season, I challenged him to take his off-season hitting to the next level by using imagery of every away park he was going to visit that season. With this approach, we tried to make his practice as game-like as possible. During indoor batting practice, he would mentally picture the opposing pitcher and surroundings, while focusing on one particular area of his swing. He would challenge himself and set specific execution goals while in the cage. After doing this intentional imagery and goal setting during practice for several weeks, he noticed his concentration and execution improve. When he later went to work with his personal hitting coach, his coach said, "I have never seen your swing or focus ever look this good." Since this was my first off-season with this athlete, we are both excited to see his higher level of preparation improve his confidence and performance during games, also.

LIKE THIS EXAMPLE, HOW CAN YOU TAKE YOUR PRACTICE GAME TO THE NEXT LEVEL?

The moral of all of these stories: Give the same value in practice as you do games. Why? Because excellence is obtained through hours of deliberate practice. Talent simply is not enough.

Learn from the stories I shared earlier...like how we had to commit as a team in order to turn our program around at WSU. How JaMarcus Russell was a flop because of a lack of sacrifice. How my teammate Jay Miller, despite his size, set the record for most career hits at WSU because of his relentless commitment to perfecting his swing. How Andy Grammer had to fail over and over again to improve his skills until he made it big. And how the power of habit impacted Fred Taylor's performance and payday.

If you want to be clutch and perform in a flow state, you have to earn it. Once you've put in the required number of hours to be a master at your craft, you'll earn credibility with your internal dialogue, which makes all the difference in increasing confidence and lowering performance anxiety.

The other important piece of putting in the work with your preparation is setting the foundation for your process. How can you trust your process when you haven't developed one? When you've put in the needed hours and appropriate repetitions, you are programming your subconscious to trust your training and to simply let go and play free of thought. That's the goal.

Remember:

- Negative thoughts are bad.
- Positive thoughts are good.
- No thoughts are best.

143

The last piece of knowledge I'll pass along to improve your performance is that there are no "big moments." Many great competitors—ranging from a variety of sports and fields of high performance—echo this approach of emphasizing practice.

Every rep, practice, training session, scrimmage, pre-season game, regular season game, post-season game, and clutch moment *should be treated the same.*

Each moment is special and important in and of itself. Just know that you are not defined by one moment, but a collection of moments. Your response and growth is more important than your failure.

When you practice that way, and put the same value on practice as you do when you compete in games, you'll be well on your way to performing as your best self.

While this chapter was all about *earning it,* in Chapter 6, we'll dig deeper into how to improve your inner-dialogue, use imagery to enhance performance, and learn how detrimental negative thoughts can be.

BREAK THE CHAINS

Have you ever been to the circus? If so, you most likely have seen at least one large elephant who is trained to do miraculous tricks. Let me tell you the story of a similar elephant named Andy.

Andy was one of the most popular and entertaining acts in the circus. After completing his eye-popping performances of throwing footballs with his trunk, sitting down on benches, and rolling on barrels, he would rest in the corner of the ring. His ringmaster would then tie a small piece of rope attached to a wooden stake in the ground around Andy's leg. Once in that position, Andy would sit still and never try to move from that spot.

How was that possible? Didn't Andy know that he had more than enough power to break free from a little piece of wood in the dirt?

Andy had been conditioned to believe that he did not not have enough strength. That negative mental conditioning began as a youngster. At an early age, Andy's ringmaster tied the young elephant up, and little Andy fought and fought with all of his might to break free. All of this effort went to waste. He simply was not strong enough yet to

145

break the rope.

With each new day, Andy tried and tried to no avail. His spirit and will eventually broke, and he gave up the fight. As he continued to grow and become stronger and more powerful, he did not even attempt to break free. His self-image and inner confidence believed that he lacked the strength and skill to free himself.*

This unhealthy self-image can be summed up with this statement: "If you think you can or you can't, you're right."

WHAT ASPECT OF YOUR LIFE HAVE YOU LET HOLD YOU DOWN LIKE ANDY THE ELEPHANT?

WHAT CHAINS OF PAST MISTAKES OR FUTURE FEARS CONTINUE TO LIMIT YOUR POTENTIAL?

It's time to break free from those chains. You have endless power within you. Make today the day where you take the first of many steps to break those chains. Right now, begin what you'll wish you would have started one year, five years, or maybe even ten years from now. Do not waste a minute. It's time to reshape your self-image and take action. Unlike Andy, with the right mindset, you can break away from your own internal chains and be like musical protege Shawn Mendes and sing, "There's nothing holdin' me back!"

(*For the record, no elephants were harmed in the making of this story. I love elephants, they are so cute!)

CHAPTER 6

ADVERTISE

YOU ARE THE AUTHOR AND NARRATOR OF THE STORY IN YOUR MIND

During my senior year, I was the vice president of a leadership team within the WSU Athletic Department called the Student-Athlete Advisory Committee (SAAC), which is a group that has representation on college campuses across the country. As committee members, we met regularly to discuss ways to enhance the student-athlete experience. Every sport on campus had (and still has) at least one SAAC representative.

During that fall, we were coming up with ideas to bring all the teams together to do a fun activity to improve culture and connection. We decided to host a talent show. Each team was responsible to submit at least one entry as an individual or group. We also created a panel of judges that consisted of a few coaches and support staff.

Being in a leadership position within SAAC, I felt like I needed to step up and enter the talent show. I also was heavily encouraged by my friends within the group because they knew I loved music and was a good dancer. When we played Purdue in the Sun Bowl, one of the events leading up to the game was a talent show, where both teams competed against each other. I did an impersonation of Michael Jackson, and people loved it. Word spread among the athletic department that "C-Hen's got moves."

Our SAAC president and volleyball captain, Holly Harris, said, "So Collin, you know you have to enter the talent show, right? We need you. It would encourage others to sign up as well."

I said, "Don't worry, Holly," with a sense of nervousness. "Sign me up."

After leaving that conversation I remember thinking I know I should do this, but we are in the middle of football season. *How am I going to put something together and practice a routine? I don't have time for this.*

I was coming off of a collarbone injury. We were ranked third in the country and were embarking on one of the greatest seasons in Cougar Football history. A lot was on the line to close out the season. To add to the challenge, the talent show was scheduled on the same week as one of the biggest games of the season, the Apple Cup (our annual game versus our arch rivals, the University of Washington Huskies).

This is the worst timing, I thought.

Several days passed since my conversation with Holly, and I had yet to plan what I was going to do for the show. We had just beaten Arizona State University at home, and the talent show was just two weeks away. I knew I didn't want to embarrass myself and do something lame.

Finally, an idea popped into my head. I came up with a plan. I was a big fan of Justin Timberlake at the time (still am). I knew all of his songs and decided to incorporate his music into my routine. Knowing who the judges were going to be, I created a backstory that one of the track coaches had left me for another guy, and I was moving on to another girl, none other than Sho-Poe, our head cook at the athletes' Cougar Fitness Cafe—a sweet little lady whom everyone loved.

Then reality set in. *This is going to be awesome,* I thought. *But wait. How am I going to practice?*

I knew I didn't have time to physically rehearse my routine since it was November and we had our final stretch of regular season games coming up. So by default, I came up with another strategy. Before going to bed each night, I would listen to Timberlake's song "Like I Love You," and mentally rehearse my moves. I created a dance routine in my mind and would see and feel my choreography mentally and physically. For two weeks, I'd lie in my bed before I went to sleep at night, and I would practice my routine in my mind.

I broke down the song into a few different parts and created moves for each section—the opening, body, bridge, chorus, rap part, and the end. I would sing and b-box in the opening and then transition to the song and execute my routine. I asked a few of my teammates to come out and break it down and dance during the rap part at the end.

During those two weeks, I didn't do one repetition physically. I would simply close my eyes, listen to the music, and see myself performing in sync (hey, I had to sneak it in) with the music. I would see my body move in my mind, and feel each move, step, and turn with my body—all while lying still in my bed. I rehearsed this way over and over and over again.

When it came time to perform on the night of the talent show, I was the last to perform. Several minutes before it was time for me to do my thing, I ran upstairs to the men's bathroom and simply did one physical rehearsal of the chorus. I tweaked one move and that was it.

151

In front of nearly four hundred of my fellow athletes, staff, and other students, I crushed my routine. All of my visualization and mental rehearsals paid off. Not only did I put on a show, but I got a standing ovation and took home the winning prize. Without practicing my entire routine one time physically—but nearly one hundred times mentally—my body couldn't tell the difference. I executed flawlessly, and I won the competition.

Like this story illustrates, the mind is very powerful. According to the Seattle Seahawks' sports psychologist, Dr. Michael Gervais, "When you mentally rehearse an activity, you create a mental groove for your brain."

By using vivid imagery, feeling my body move, and seeing my routine mentally before it happened, I established a neural-pathway, or groove, in my brain that my body played out when it was time to perform.

Similar to this example, this chapter is all about giving you the mental tools to perform at your highest level. I share stories on how self-talk, visualizing, and taking control of your internal dialogue are key components of accessing flow.

Energy Flows Where Focus Goes
Our brain is a magnet. What we think about and focus on oftentimes manifests itself in our lives. This concept is sometimes called the Law of Attraction. As in, we attract what we think about the most. Here is a catch phrases that help explain this phenomenon:

Thoughts become things.

CAN YOU THINK ABOUT A TIME WHEN YOU ACHIEVED SOME-THING GREAT...WHEN YOU HAD A POSITIVE MINDSET AND BE-LIEVED 100 PERCENT IN YOUR HEART THAT SOMETHING GOOD WAS GOING TO HAPPEN?

CAN YOU REMEMBER A TIME WHEN ALL YOU THOUGHT ABOUT WAS ACHIEVING A SPECIFIC GOAL AND YOU WOULD VISUALIZE YOURSELF DOING THAT ACTIVITY OR ACHIEVING THAT GOAL?

You may have heard of the phrase, "You can do anything you put your mind to." That's just another way of describing the impact of our thought life.

Having optimism, focusing on positive events in your life, and believing they will come true creates a powerful force for your subconscious. Conversely, when you are a pessimist, and focus on negative outcomes, you often attract those very events. (Remember the Mind Over Matter piece earlier in this book featuring football player Nathaniel Holcomb attacking his fear?).

For example, have you ever been asked to grab the salt (or something similar) in the kitchen pantry or cabinet, and you say to yourself over and over again, "I can't find it. I can't find it. I can't find it." After much searching (and repeating that negative statement to yourself) you can't find what you were asked to look for. Then you ask for help, and the other person finds it in two seconds.

This is the power of the brain. It can be our biggest strength or biggest weakness in attracting the outcomes we seek (like finding the salt or winning the game).

To help athletes, sales professionals, performers, and peo-

153

ple take better control of their mindset and thoughts, I teach a mental map system that helps keep the brain on the right track. This system serves as an internal filter to recognize negative thoughts and helps people snap their mental images back to the positive. I call this mental system and process "Think Above the Line."

Think Above the Line

Did you know that we have thirty-five automatic thoughts per minute? Some research suggests that we say three hundred to one thousand words to ourselves every minute, also. Our brain never shuts off. One of the skills that elite performers have is the ability to limit the time they dwell or worry about future failures. The fact is, having negative thoughts pop into our head is perfectly normal. Even the elites like MLB Los Angeles Angels' all-star Mike Trout and WNBA Seattle Storm's Sue Bird are not immune to these natural human emotions.

The goal is to be able to recognize these thoughts and understand that this is not the real you. This is your inner-critic. We all have this internal judge that tries to sabotage our performance by comparing, worrying about opinions, and chasing the lie of perfection. The aim is to be your true, authentic, creative self and filter out these thoughts and get back into a positive or neutral mindset.

We have two mindsets: The *critic* and the *creative*. See the diagram on the right.

CRITIC VS. CREATIVE BRAIN

CRITIC	CREATIVE
PESSIMISTIC	OPTIMISTIC
COMPARES	CARES
INSECURE	CONFIDENT
VALIDATION IN OUTCOMES	VALIDATION IN EFFORT
AFRAID TO FAIL	SEES FAILURE AS GROWTH
OVER FOCUS OF SELF	UNSELFISH
PAST/FUTURE FOCUSED	IN THE NOW
CLOSE-MINDED	OPEN-MINDED

WHAT MINDSET DO YOU HAVE?

Take a moment and reflect on a time when you were performing at your absolute best. What were your thoughts like? Odds are you didn't have very many thoughts. Here's the deal: *Negative thoughts are bad. Positive thoughts are good.* The peak mental state, though, is to have no thought. That's when we are in a flow state—no judgment, no stress, but pure enjoyment and confidence.

155

So how do you get there and operate in your creative brain? By learning how to "Think Above the Line," or "**TATL**," for short.

THINK **ABOVE** THE LINE

POSITIVE

CONFIDENCE	OPTIMISM
PAST SUCCESS	BEST CASE SCENARIOS
HOW YOU'VE *EARNED* IT	"DO"
SOMEONE WHO BELIEVES IN YOU	SELF-BELIEF
PAST FAILURES	WORST CASE SCENARIOS
REGRETTING WHAT YOU DIDN'T DO	"DON'T DO"
LISTENING TO HATERS	SELF-DOUBT
SHAME	PESSIMISM

PAST

FUTURE

NEGATIVE

Think back to when you were a young child. Did you ever tattle to an adult on a sibling or one of your friends if they were doing something that negatively impacted or harmed you?

This is a similar idea. Instead of telling your mom, dad, or teacher, you are using your conscious brain to tell your subconscious brain that something is keeping you from achieving your goals. With this system, you will become more aware when your sabotaging thoughts appear.

Think of your brain as having four corners, kind of like the game of four square you may have played in elementary school.

The top half represents positive thoughts and the bottom half represents negative thoughts. The left side represents your past, while the right side represents your future. The middle line that separates the top and bottom halves represents your brain's internal filter. If individuals have a dirty or broken filter, they are spending most of their thought life replaying past failures and worrying about what bad things might happen in the future.
Let's break down these four corners.

Bottom Left (Past Negative)

Past Failures
Individuals who are stuck thinking in the bottom left of the TATL diagram find themselves dwelling on the past and reliving past failures. They allow past negative outcomes to shape their internal story.

Here's an example: During game one of the 1995 NBA Finals, Orlando Magic shooting guard Nick Anderson stepped up to the free throw line with ten seconds left in the game, hopeful to add to their three-point lead versus the Houston

Rockets. If he could just make one free throw, he would seal the game for the Magic. Unfortunately, he missed both free throws, but on his second miss, he miraculously got his own rebound and was fouled again. When he lined up to take two more free throws, the pressure and moment got the best of this sharp-shooter, whose career free throw percentage was just under 80 percent. He missed those two free throws again, and when the Rockets got the rebound, they went down to the other end of the court and tied the game with a clutch shot at the buzzer. This made shot forced overtime. The Rockets ended up winning that game and sweeping the Magic in four games.

That experience haunted Anderson for the rest of his career. An excellent free throw shooter up to that point, his percentage dropped to 40 percent after that moment. He couldn't shake that mistake, and that experience greatly affected his ability to perform for the rest of his career.

HAVE YOU EVER LET A PAST MISTAKE NEGATIVELY AFFECT YOUR PERFORMANCE? DO YOU EVER REPLAY A PAST MISTAKE OVER AND OVER AGAIN?

Haters
Another hurdle for individuals who are operating in the bottom left of the TATL matrix is being overly consumed by haters and criticizers. Some performers allow negative feedback to affect their performance. These individuals allow someone else's opinion of them to shape their own internal opinion. This negative internal story impedes their ability to perform in a flow state and at their peak in future competitions.

An example that comes to mind is the promising, yet short,

career of the 1998 second overall NFL draft pick, Ryan Leaf. In the locker room after game three of Leaf's first season with the San Diego Chargers, a reporter asked him about his poor performance. Leaf infamously exploded and yelled at the reporter, and it was all caught on camera. The footage of this public explosion went viral. This was the beginning of the end for him. Insecurities, immaturity, and self-sabotaging behavior shortened Leaf's career to only four seasons.

You must understand that having haters is a part of being a top performer. Don't let someone else's opinion of you shape how you see yourself. Remember to go back to your MVPs (revert back to Chapter 4 on Vision) and stay true to your values and mission.

It's unfortunate, but we live in a selfish and insecure society. If you are balling, you are going to have supporters as much as you are going to have haters. Haters come with the territory. Celebrities from LeBron James to Lady Gaga all have a legion of haters. Pay them no mind. Stay focused on your process and what you can control.

HAVE YOU EVER HAD SOMEONE CRITICIZE YOUR GAME, WHICH YOU LET HINDER PERFORMANCE? HOW DID YOU HANDLE IT?

Top Left (Past Positive)

Unlike my example of how Nick Anderson dwelled on his four consecutive missed free throws in game one of the NBA Finals (which negatively impacted his shooting for the rest of his career), true champions are able to shift their mindset away from failure and spend more of their mental energy on more productive thoughts. There are several areas one can focus on to keep their mind in a more positive state than reliving past failures.

It is critical to develop internal trust with yourself as a competitor. By putting in the necessary work, replaying past successes, and focusing on the support of those who care about you, you will utilize the mindset needed to perform at your best. This is a form of self-advertising.

Similar to how companies advertise their products or services to consumers, we need to advertise to ourselves that we have what it takes to be a champion. How do you do that? I'll explain.

Past Success
In Super Bowl XLIX, the Seattle Seahawks were one yard and one play away from securing their second world championship in two years. New England Patriots rookie cornerback Malcolm Butler, however, stepped in front of wide receiver Ricardo Lockette on a slant pattern and intercepted star quarterback Russell Wilson's pass. Butler's amazingly clutch play secured another Super Bowl championship to add to the storied Patriot franchise (including a huge celebration by the players and coaches on the sideline). While the Pats were partying, the Seahawks' sidelines and entire fanbase were crushed.

HAS AN EVENT LIKE THIS EVER HAPPENED TO YOU? IF SO, HOW DID YOU RESPOND?

Being so close, yet walking away in defeat due to his mistake, could have left Wilson second-guessing his abilities. But this is why clutch performers like Wilson are ballers. The best of the best are on another level because of their ability to respond to failure and shorten the time to recovery. Instead of dwelling on this mistake, Wilson had other plans. Since 2012, and up to that point, no other quarterback in the NFL has led their team to more fourth-quarter or overtime come-from-behind wins than Russell. Wilson's mental performance coach, Trevor Moawad, put together a highlight film of every single one of Wilson's late-game come-from-behind victories in his career. Instead of replying this one Super Bowl mistake, Wilson focused on replaying where he was at his best.

The strategy paid off. The following season, Wilson set franchise records for passing yards (4,024), passing touchdowns (34), and passer rating (110.1). He even led the NFL with the highest passer rating and was selected to his third consecutive Pro Bowl.

Where Nick Anderson let his finals failure negatively impact his future performance, Wilson used his failure as fuel and motivation to get better and even improve his performance. A trick to help him do this was revisiting and replaying when he was at his best.

THINK OF MOMENTS WHEN YOU HAD SUCCESS AND WERE PERFORMING AT YOUR BEST. MENTALLY FILE THESE MEMORIES OR WRITE THEM DOWN. USE THESE EXPERIENCES AS A FORM OF ADVERTISING TO YOUR SUBCONSCIOUS THAT YOU GOT THIS! USE THESE MEMORIES ESPECIALLY AFTER MOMENTS WHEN YOU FAIL.

Earned It
Like I explained in Chapter 6, one of the most effective ways to tap into the power of flow is to put in enough hours of practice and effort to improve your skills. Performing at an elite level requires an elite level of preparation. Whether

it's tackling a huge wave or skateboard ramp, or playing in a big football or baseball game, if you haven't earned the right to be great (by putting in the work to master your skills), you don't deserve to be great.

To help quiet your doubt and inner critic before and during competition, take a moment to replay all the hours, practices, and hard work you put into to get to where you are. This should help increase your confidence that you're ready and deserving of being an elite performer.

Please note: This mental strategy only works if you have actually put in the work!

Someone Who Believes in You
Instead of focusing on the haters and people who say you aren't good enough (like my Ryan Leaf example), focus your energy on at least one person who believes and cares about you.

The strategy worked for Olympic medalist and swimming champion Janet Evans. Before competing in her first Olympics in 1988, Evans felt very stressed and was second-guessing if she belonged or had what it took to be an Olympian. Luckily, she received support from one of the top Olympic swimmers of all time, Mark Spitz (eleven medals, including nine golds), who gave her a pep talk to get her mind back on track. He said he believed in her and that he was really impressed with her abilities. This former world record holder in seven events said that he was going to cheer her on during the entire competition.

Evans said that this encouragement helped relieve some of her stress. Instead of focusing on people, media, or critics that said she was too inexperienced, too small, or too young to win (entering the 1988 Seoul, South Korea Olympics, Evans had just turned eighteen years old, was a mere five-foot-four and ninety-nine pounds), she focused on the encouragement and belief from Spitz. With this focus, she went on to win three individual gold medals.

In my opinion, in a way, having haters is a good thing. It means you're doing something. Instead of thinking about people who say you can't, focus on just one person who thinks you can. Because in the end, it takes only one scout, one team, or one coach to like you and give you an opportunity.

WHO IS ONE PERSON IN YOUR LIFE THAT TRULY CARES AND BELIEVES IN YOU? FOCUS ON THIS SUPPORT INSTEAD OF OBSESSING ON THE "HATERS" DURING TIMES OF WORRY OR STRESS.

Bottom Right (Future Negative)

Worst-Case Scenarios
The power of thought works both in the positive and negative. If you obsess over bad things happening, if you give your energy to negativity, if you picture worst-case scenarios happening to you, you are simply feeding your subconscious to bring those events to life. Positive thinking doesn't always work, but negative thinking always works...for the negative. An example of this is the story of Bill Buckner.

In 1986, Boston Red Sox first baseman Bill Buckner made one of the most famous errors in the history of Major League Baseball. It was game six of the World Series, and the Red Sox were leading the New York Mets by two runs in the bottom of the ninth inning. With two runners on base, all Boston had to do was get one more out, and they would erase their seven-decade World Series Championship drought. The Mets' Mookie Wilson was at the plate and hit a chopping ground ball down the right side, toward first base. Buckner, the sure-handed all-star first baseman (and one-time batting champion), charged it, but the ball snuck passed his glove like it had a pair of eyes. With the ball rolling into right field, both Mets players crossed home plate to tie the game. The Red Sox ended up losing both game six and seven of the World Series to the Mets.

Boston fans blamed Buckner for the loss. His life forever changed after that unfortunate moment. What's most interesting was what Buckner prophetically said just days before that fateful game six. While speaking with a reporter during batting practice, Buckner said, "The dreams are that you're gonna have a great series and win. The nightmares are that you're gonna let the winning run score on a ground ball through your legs.[...]"

Say what?

By projecting a worst-case scenario, Buckner's greatest fear happened to him.

ARE YOU THINKING IN BEST-CASE OR WORST-CASE SCENARIOS? IS THERE A TIME WHEN YOU KEPT THINKING ABOUT SOMETHING NOT HAPPENING AND IT HAPPENED?

"Don't Do"
As a young pitcher in the Atlanta Braves organization, Tom Glavine was having a rough time adjusting to the high level of talent and skill of professional hitters. With the pressure of being a high draft pick, Glavine spent most of his mental energy on not screwing up. His self-talk centered around avoiding failure, starting each goal by saying, "don't do...."

Glavine's internal dialogue sounded like this:

- Don't leave the ball up.
- Don't walk this batter.
- Don't give up a homerun.
- Don't lose the game.

This negative thought process of avoiding instead of attacking, impeded Glavine's ability to actualize his true potential and perform at his best.

Here is a different example: When I say, "Don't think of a white bear. Don't think of a white bear. Don't think of a white bear." What are you thinking about? My guess is a white bear.

When you use words internally like "don't do," or "avoid," and think of worst-case scenarios, you are actually attracting those events in your life. The brain cannot identify the word "don't." It only sees the image or action you are avoiding.

Top Right (Positive Future)

"Do"
With help from one of his coaches, Glavine was able to make a basic mental shift. Avoiding negative outcomes wasn't working, so Glavine changed one simple word internally. Instead of saying "don't do," Glavine began to say "do" before each objective. His new self-talk sounded like this:

- Do keep the ball down.
- Do strike the hitter out.
- Do get a ground ball.
- Do win the game.

This simple mental shift of picturing what outcomes he desired, instead of imagining what events he didn't want, made a huge impact on his performance. Glavine used this imagery technique to have a twenty-year big league career

165

including two Cy Young Awards, nine all-star appearances, and two World Series rings.

A lesson from Glavine: Before each game and each play, picture what you want to happen instead of what you don't want to happen. Start each mental sentence with the word "do," instead of "don't do."

Best-Case Scenarios
As a young high school wrestler, all Colton Tracy wanted was to be a state champion. He worked tirelessly on his body and skills to be the best. All of his hard work, however, still left him short of his goal. During his freshman, sophomore, and junior seasons, he made it all the way to the final match of the state championships, but lost every time. He was so close to his goal, but Tracy kept falling short.

Going into his senior year, he wasn't going to let a loss in the finals happen again. Before the season started, Tracy did some serious mental work to harness the power of his subconscious. He grabbed a sheet of paper and wrote down this sentence more than twenty times: *I will be a state champion on February 22, 2014.*

With his Bonney Lake High School logo in the backdrop, Tracy printed out on a piece of paper: *I WILL WIN STATE.*

Tracy took it a step further and drew a picture of himself on the wrestling mat on his knees with his hands in the air celebrating his title. He even drew the Tacoma Dome, the location of the state wrestling tournament, in the background.

After the final match of the state tournament, a photographer snapped a picture of Tracy celebrating his championship.

He finally did it! He won the state title!

You might not believe this if you didn't see it for yourself, but the photograph looks identical to the one that Tracy drew before the season.

By thinking in best-case scenarios and visualizing his goal before it happened, Tracy actualized his dream.

HOW CAN YOU APPLY COLTON TRACY'S STORY TO ATTRACT MORE SUCCESS IN YOUR LIFE? SUGGESTION: MAKE A DREAM BOARD (LIKE TRACY DID) OF AN IMAGE OR IMAGES OF WHAT YOU'D LIKE TO ACCOMPLISH.

Visualization
Every morning on game day, Memphis Grizzlies all-star point guard Mike Conley lies in bed, closes his eyes, and visualizes his performance before it happens. He creates mental images of the arena, the court, and executing the offense. He mentally rehearses his shots going in all over the court. This strategy has helped Conley become one of the highest-paid players in the NBA.

"When I don't take time to visualize," Conley told author and entrepreneur Lewis Howes in the *School of Greatness* podcast, "I feel off and usually don't play as well."

Whether it's Conley's example, or my previously mentioned talent show illustration, using mental imagery really works. But, why is this? Let me explain.

The brain thinks in pictures, not in words. When you visualize an action, this activates the same areas of the brain as actually doing that action. For example, when you men-

167

tally picture shooting a basketball, you stimulate the same part of the brain that is activated when you actually shoot a ball. For instance, stroke victims who lose function of an arm can stimulate blood flow to that area, just by imagining they are moving their arm.

Whether we visualize it or learn something new, our brain forms new neural connections that create a mental map or groove. The more we mentally rehearse these actions, the stronger the connections become.

When you visualize an event or movement (also called a "neural pathway") your brain is creating a roadmap for your body to follow. According to many psychologists, the more senses (smell, sound, feel, taste, sight, etc.) you can incorporate while you visualize, the better. By using imagery, neurons that fire together wire together and form a pathway for the brain to execute.

These mental rehearsals have the power to actually reshape our brain through something called "neuroplasticity." Through mindfulness, visualization, and meditation practices, we can literally rebuild our brain.

RAS

When you have a clear picture of what you want, you're doing your subconscious a favor. This is where the Reticular Activating System (RAS) comes into play. The RAS is located at the core of your brain stem and serves as a mental filter. It takes instructions from your conscious mind and passes them onto your subconscious mind. Your RAS helps the brain stay focused on what it needs to do to achieve the desired goal and keep blinders on less important factors that will not help the subconscious achieve its desired vision.

For example, a mother with a crying newborn baby in the other room is able to filter out the TV, the neighbor mowing the lawn, and her other loud children to hear her baby waking from a nap. The RAS is like a heat-seeking missile to help your brain stay on target.

Below are several examples of visualization and the power of mental rehearsal and activating the brain's RAS.

James Nesmeth

- Major James Nesmeth was a combat pilot who loved to play golf. He was not particularly good at golf; Nesmeth typically shot in the mid-nineties.
- During his Vietnam wartime duty, his plane was shot down over North Vietnam, and he was a prisoner of war for seven years.
- During that seven years he experienced sleep deprivation, torture, and long stretches of solitary confinement. To keep sane, Nesmeth envisioned playing an eighteen-hole golf course. With unlimited time, he would visualize every nuance—his grip, the feel of the grass, the club hitting the ball, weather conditions, and approaching each shot.
- When Nesmeth was freed, he went through rehabilitation, and the first time he played golf he shot a seventy-four! Even though his body and physical health declined, his mental game improved...so much so he cut twenty shots off his score—all while not even picking up a club for seven years.

Free Throws

- A study conducted by Dr. Judd Biasiotto at the University of Chicago showed the power of visualization. He gathered individuals and split them into three groups and tested each group on how many free throws they could make.
- After this, he had the first group practice free throws every day for an hour. The second group didn't physically shoot, but would simply visualize themselves making

169

free throws. The third group did not shoot or visualize.
- After thirty days, he tested them again. As expected, by doing nothing, the third group did not improve their free throw percentage. The first group, that practiced shooting at the gym, improved by 24 percent. And what is astonishing, the second group that simply visualized, improved its accuracy by 23 percent without touching a basketball!
- This study made a powerful point that by using imagery, you can improve your skills.

Ray Allen
- Miami Heat Head Coach Erik Spoelstra wasn't surprised when his all-star forward Ray Allen hit one of the most clutch shots in NBA history.
- Facing elimination versus the San Antonio Spurs in game six of the 2014 NBA Finals, Allen scrambled to the right corner, tightroped between the three-point line and out of bounds, and drilled the game-tying shot to force overtime.
- The Heat went on to win the game and the series. What's interesting is that Spoelstra often wondered why, after most practices, Allen would lie on his back under the hoop with his eyes closed. He would then jump to his feet and scramble to catch and shoot a corner three.
- Spoelstra concluded, nothing happens by accident. Allen rehearsed that game-winner a thousand times—mentally and physically.

Virtual Workouts
- The Cleveland Clinic Foundation exercise psychologist Guang Yue studied and compared people who worked out at a gym versus people who did virtual workouts mentally.
- He found a 30 percent muscle increase in the group that went to the gym, while the group of participants who did mental weight training exercises, increased

muscle strength by almost half as much (13.5 percent).

- This average remained for three months following the mental training, showing it's possible you can make your muscles stronger with your brain!

The evidence is clear: Take your game to the next level by not only using your body, but by giving your brain visual reps, also. Utilize the power of visualization and be clutch like the individuals mentioned above.

WHEN CAN YOU CARVE OUT A FEW MINUTES EACH DAY TO VISU-ALIZE YOUR GOALS?

Take a moment right now and visualize yourself making highlights in your sport. Don't just see yourself make plays...feel it too. **Tip**: Add your favorite music to help alter your mental state while visualizing.

I suggest that you use visualization as a consistent tool before competition and even before each play.

Mindfulness
The act of mindfulness is a growing practice. From yoga classes to meditation centers to guided visualization exercises, the positive evidence of putting away your electronics, unplugging, and getting centered quietly with your breath and brain has many proven benefits.

So what exactly is *"mindfulness?"* Here's a quick definition courtesy of the *Merriam-Webster Online Dictionary:*

noun
(1) the quality or state of being mindful;

171

(2) the practice of maintaining a nonjudgmental state of heightened or complete awareness of one's thoughts, emotions, or experiences on a moment-to-moment basis; also: such a state of awareness.

My definition of mindfulness is getting centered, focusing on one thing (whether your breath, a word, a sound, or object), and allowing your brain to quiet the noise. When an errant thought pops up, recognize it, and go back to your one thing (like your breath or mantra). When you do that, it's like taking a mental rep for your brain...just like doing a rep of curls to strengthen your biceps.

From Fortune 500 companies to Olympic and professional athletes, to schools, singers, and actors—mindfulness, meditation, and visualization are being utilized as not only a stress reliever, but as a performance enhancer, as well.

Some say that prayer is *asking*, where having a mindfulness practice is *listening*.

We all have wisdom within us. By having a mindfulness practice (whether you set an intention or not beforehand), you will be more likely to uncover ideas, inspiration, and clarity.

The legendary Oprah Winfrey once said, "Meditate. Breathe consciously. Listen. Pay attention. Treasure every moment and make the connection."

Here's another way of looking at the power of mindfulness.

During stressful moments like giving a speech, or competing in an important game, it might feel like being in a storm. In this storm, there is heavy wind and the rain is coming down from all sides. People in the streets are frantically running all over the place trying to find shelter. Moments like this often times create worry, panic, and alter our physical state (elevated heart rate, sweating, shallow breathing, etc.).

Practicing meditation or some form of mindfulness will help get you out of the storm. Instead of being in the street, taking on the craziness all around you, you will now be inside; in a safe building with a glass window watching all of the chaos outside. The storm doesn't go away, but you are able to sit back and watch it in a state of peace and calm. During that speech, you will be focusing on your necessary keys to give a fantastic presentation. In a crucial moment in a game, you'll be able to have more clarity on what you need to do to execute (instead of focusing on what could go wrong). By having practiced a consistent form of mindfulness, you will be more in the *now* (not worrying about the past or future). This skillset will deeply help you when "Mr. Worry" (as my five-year-old son calls it) pops up in your head.

OK, enough about storms and rain. So why else is practicing some form of mindfulness important as a performer—especially as part of your preparation?

Here's my opinion: Stress is inevitable no matter what sport you play, your experience level, or age. At some point during the season or a game (and life), there will be a stress trigger, whether it is a tie score with little time on the clock...your starting position on the line...failing...your number being called and an expectation for you to deliver results...or you just feel that everyone is watching you...the question isn't "if," it's "when" will these stressful moments come?

When you practice mindfulness, you access a small area of your brain that I call the C-Spot. The "C" is short for clarity and calm. The more you practice mindfulness the larger that spot becomes and the easier you will be able to access not only clarity and calm during pressure situations, but you will discover more awareness and wisdom.

How will you quiet your mind and get your brain back on track? If you haven't practiced some form of mindfulness as part of your preparation, performing at your peak will be much harder. Worse yet, the moment might get too big for you. Instead of focusing on your breath or one thought (whether it's your pitch thought, swing thought, or shot thought—I'll explain these concepts in more detail later in this chapter), your mind is at risk of being overly cluttered, and your performance will suffer.

To help you get more centered, relaxed, and focused, below are five simple steps you can use to practice mindfulness each day. This system helps prime your mind and body to work as one. I call this "Five to Thrive." It takes just five minutes each day to practice these five simple steps. For each step, allow one minute to complete.

Five to Thrive

1. **Focus on your breath**—Relax your mind and relax your body by focusing on your breath. To begin, breathe in through your nose and out through your mouth. Once you've done that at least three times, go back to your normal breath. With each exhale scan your body to make sure all muscles and body parts are free from tension
2. **Focus on gratitude**—Take a moment to run through all the things in your life for which you are grateful. Gratitude reduces the stress hormone cortisol and is the foundation of peace.
3. **Focus on times when you were in the zone**—Replay images and moments when you were performing at your very best. "Re-feel" what those moments felt like.
4. **Focus how you have earned it**—Think about all the

174

time, energy, and practice you have put into your craft.
Replay all the hours you have put into earning the right
to be at this place.

5. **Visualize yourself achieving your objective and goals**—Imagine in vivid detail what you are wearing, what you see, what you feel, what you hear, and who is around you. Create a mental highlight reel of yourself performing at your best.

To cool down or complete this exercise, finish by taking as long as you'd like to simply focus on your breath. When an errant thought pops up, it's perfectly normal and OK. Simply recognize it and come back to your breath. This will be a great practice to help you quiet the noise in the future (especially during stressful moments in life and competition). The act of coming away from that thought, and back to your breath, is the brain's mental rep (like taking a repetition in the batting cage). That is the exercise that trains the brain to quiet the noise.

Here's a quote from successful Hollywood actor Hugh Jackman on the power of mindfulness: "Meditation is all about the pursuit of nothingness. It's like the ultimate rest. It's better than the best sleep you've ever had. It's a quieting of the mind. It sharpens everything, especially your appreciation of your surroundings. It keeps life fresh."

If it works for a media mogul like Oprah and a tough action hero like Jackman, maybe you should carve out quiet time each day to be still and connect with your breath and body. Sometimes, less is more.

Tip: Download the app *Headspace*. The first ten sessions (only ten minutes each session) are free and the app does a great job of introducing how and why meditation is important. Another mindfulness app I like is *Oak - Meditation & Breathing.*

WHEN WILL YOU SCHEDULE AND EXECUTE YOUR DAILY MINDFUL-
NESS PRACTICE?

One Thought
The *Five to Thrive* exercise is a phenomenal tool to prime
your mind and body BEFORE performing. But what about
DURING the game? Picking one physical key or objective
and simply focusing on that one thought and feeling is a
strategy that is similar to having one mantra word that you
focus on and repeat while meditating. This approach will
help quiet the noise in your brain, while visualizing a mental groove for your subconscious and body to follow.

All-time tennis champion Serena Williams uses a similar
system. Before each tennis match, she writes down her objective for that competition on a notecard (possible examples: "move your feet," "quiet head," "follow through," etc.).
During game and set breaks, this multiple Olympic and
Grand Slam champion pulls out her notecard to remind
her of what she needs to focus on. This one mental and
physical objective comes from what she worked on during
her training for that tournament (Williams also writes positive affirmations on her notecard).

I once heard mental conditioning coach Trevor Moawad
share a story about Olympic champion and once the fast-
est man alive, Michael Johnson. Moawad said Johnson
kept it simple during his world record performance at the
1996 Olympics. The American sprinting great told himself
four simple statements that would help him carry over his
training to competition:
* Head down.
* Pump your arms.
* Explode.
* **Be a bullet.**

176

This simple imagery—*be a bullet*—helped Johnson narrow his focus to win the gold and set the world record in the 200-meter dash with a time of 19.32.

Like Johnson, I remember a baseball tournament I played in during high school in which I had a single focus that helped me dominate. While hitting .800 for the tournament, I recall that the only thing I said to myself was "hands back." I said those words internally and felt the feeling of my hands being back in the proper load position. This basic mental approach helped me quiet the storm around me and simplify my technique.

HOW CAN YOU USE THIS ONE THOUGHT APPROACH?

Another option to quiet your mind is to count.

All-American, and later Pro Bowl football player, Reggie Bush, hit a slump returning punts at USC. He encountered a spell in which he either fumbled or dropped the ball while back in his punt-returner position. He said he couldn't stop thinking about dropping the ball.

To help quiet his mind, he began to count numbers in his head (especially when the ball was in the air: "one...two...three...four...five"). This mental approach kept his mind away from worst-case scenarios, like dropping the ball, and to a place of no thought. Bush got his brain out of his body's way. This technique allowed him to let his natural ability take over, and he never again dropped a punt in college.

Yet another option, besides counting, is music.

When working with a high school baseball player, he confessed that he had a hard time calming his nerves and quieting his thoughts while at the plate hitting (especially during the time we met). I had him try humming his favorite song quietly to himself while in the on-deck circle before walking up to the plate to hit. He gave this strategy a try and found it effective. In his second at-bat, he slammed a double off the outfield wall. With this technique, he was able to get out of his slump and out of his own head.

A final "single point of focus" option is to pick one place, location, area, or piece of equipment in the field of competition to help you stay focused and centered. Let this one image (foul pole, goal post, inspirational sign, wristband, etc.) help you get your mind back on track and in the proper perspective.

An example of using this technique is from the great Northwest. During his college career, all-time Pac-12 and WSU passing leader, Luke Falk, wore a white Nike wristband with the name "Brad" written in black marker on his left wrist during games. This was in honor of Falk's AAU and select basketball coach, Brad Barton, who tragically died of a diabetic seizure when Falk was a junior in high school. After most touchdowns and big plays, Falk could be seen touching this wristband, then pointing his fingers in the air as a salute to his fallen mentor who played an inspirational role in Falk's life. This act kept the game in perspective and helped this all-conference player compete with a sense of gratitude.

HOW DO YOU STAY CENTERED DURING COMPETITION?

These mindfulness examples will give your brain a healthy distraction from the many possible external factors that might cause you to lose your focus. Also, when you fail, instead of dwelling on your mistake, go back to your one thought or mind-quieting strategy. These approaches are much more productive than worrying about making mistakes or what others are thinking of you.

Come up with your own one thought or single point of focus strategy that you can use during competition. Write it down, tell someone. Use this as a tool to quiet the noise, increase concentration, and practice a form of mindfulness during competition.

You can do this! Use these mental tools to help lower your stress, create clarity, and increase your confidence to be authentically you. Being a champion—and more importantly, your best self—requires just as much mental work as it does physical work.

By consistently using your conscious brain to advertise to your subconscious mind that you have what it takes, while visualizing what you want to achieve creates more opportunities to perform in flow. The more you are able to operate in a state of flow, the more you will be able to unlock your full potential.

THE BREATH METHOD

Practicing mindfulness and visualization are proven to be cornerstones of peak performance. Many young athletes are missing out on this technique because of a lack of emphasis, training, and consistent implementation.

Based on feedback from coaches and players, my guided visualization sessions (like this one below) are one of the most impactful tools that have aided performance.

To help expose you to a mindfulness system, here is another simple pre-game exercise that you can do at home, during the drive to the field/court, or as part of your warm-up routine. This simple technique will help prime your mindset so you can be in a more relaxed and focused state (this takes only three to five minutes to complete). I call it the "BREATH Method."

B – BREATHE: Close your eyes, focus on your breath, and breathe in through your nose and out through your mouth. Count to five during each inhale and to five again during the exhale (controlled breathing helps lower stress hormones in our body). After at least five deep breaths, go back to a normal breathing pattern.

R – RESET: Come up with a "reset" (mantra) word that you can use to keep your mind in the game during down time, moments of stress, when you fail, or even we you succeed (examples: "believe," "confident," or "release"). Say your reset word to yourself in-between each breath or during the exhale.

Example: Inhale, count—*one...two...three...four...five*—say, "believe," exhale, count—*one...two...three...four...five.* Do this exercise at least five times.

E – EXIT: Allow yourself to exit any and all thought, doubt, and negative energy, and simply focus on your breath and/or reset word. When an errant thought pops into your head, that's OK; come back to your breath and reset word (this is taking a mental rep to strengthen the brain, much like squats for making our legs stronger).

A – AFFIRMATION: Once you have taken a minute or two to focus on your breath and reset word, identify a goal for the practice or game. Be sure to use your imagination, and visualize this goal as if it is already achieved (with as many senses as possible: sight, sound, touch, feeling, etc.). Neurons that fire together wire together, making these connections stronger. Give yourself some positive self-talk and affirmations to support these mental images. This step will help the body and subconscious mind work together. This is also called "neuroplasticity"—the ability to reshape our own brain.

TH – THANKFUL: Lastly, take a moment and think about what you are grateful for and what makes you happy. I call this a gratitude checklist (examples: faith, family, health, friends, experiences, etc.). Gratitude has been clinically proven to reduce stress by as much as 28 percent and create an optimistic and positive mindset, according to Dr. Robert Emmons of University of California, Davis.

182

To help you execute the BREATH Method, take out a piece of paper, journal, or notecard and write down a response to these three prompts:

1. *Reset word* (what's your word?)
2. *Affirmations*
   » Goal (what do you want to accomplish during competition?)
   » Positive self-talk (what are three statements that affirm why you believe you will achieve your goal?)
3. *Thankful* (what are you most grateful for?)

My advice is to keep this list with you somewhere during practices and games (similar to my earlier Serena Williams example). This tool will be of most impact if done consistently. Read it to yourself during pre-game warm-ups or even during halftime or breaks. Having a daily ritual of visualizing and activating the calming power of mindfulness will help similarly to your physical conditioning—but instead for your overall mental fitness. These principles will not only improve performance in athletics, but in school, work, social situations, and other areas of life, also.

CHAPTER 7

FEED THE GOOD WOLF

IF YOU HAVE THESE THREE, YOU WILL HAVE EVERYTHING: GRATITUDE, GROWTH, GENEROSITY

I didn't always play wide receiver. Because I had natural speed, I played the running back position in my early years of junior football. My first year of tackle football was in the first grade with the Puyallup Roughriders. I later switched to quarterback in the sixth grade. My accurate arm and running ability made me an asset for my team. I was like a mini Michael Vick. Through my entire junior high career (seventh through ninth grade) at the quarterback position, we lost only one game. With this success, I had a tough decision to make entering high school as to which position to play.

Throughout my childhood and teen years, Puyallup High School had a powerhouse football program led by Hall of Fame Head Coach Mike Huard. The Vikings won a state title and went to the state finals or semifinals multiple times under Coach Huard's leadership. Puyallup sent many players off to play at the college level and even the NFL. Not only was Coach Huard an elite coach, but he was also the father to two University of Washington record-setting quarterbacks, Damon and Brock Huard. Damon and Brock went to Puyallup High School and after their college careers played in the NFL.

The third and youngest Huard brother was my good friend, Luke. Luke played quarterback, also. Damon, Brock, and

Luke all had prototypical size and weight—ranging from six-foot-four to six-foot-five and about 225 pounds. Luke was one year ahead of me in school and already had one year as a starter under his belt. College programs were already recruiting him due to his talent, size, and lineage.

I knew if I wanted to see the field on offense, I needed to find a new position. So, entering my high school sophomore year, I moved to wide receiver and earned a starting position alongside future University of Washington standout wide receiver Todd Elstrom. We had an excellent season that year. We won our league and made a deep run into the state playoffs. I earned all-conference honors and felt very comfortable in my new position.

My mental and physical game were aligned. I remember not feeling fear of dropping a pass that entire season. I had a quiet mind that was *thinking above the line* (remember the TATL strategy?). That all changed, however, during a passing league game going into my junior season.

Every off-season, we would play in a summer passing league at the beautiful college campus of the University of Puget Sound in Tacoma. During a game that summer, I encountered a serious challenge to my healthy mindset.

It was a hot July evening. The sun was out, and you could smell the fresh-cut grass. There were many teams playing on various fields all around, and you could hear the echoes of players calling out signals and parents clapping and cheering for their teams.

During our second game, I lined up at my outside X position and ran a deep take-off route on the left sideline. I was running effortlessly like Usain Bolt, passing defensive backs. There I was, at least five yards behind the defense. It was like slow motion. I could see the ball flying in the air for what seemed like three hours instead of three seconds. With no one around me, the ball finally came down. When it touched my hands and outstretched fingers, it was like I had frying pan hands. I wasn't able to hold on, and the ball fell to the ground. I flat-out dropped it.

I remember jogging back to the huddle feeling discouraged and embarrassed I let my team down.

How did that happen? I thought, while feeling a rush of embarrassment engulf me. *I never drop passes.*

In the next series, Luke called the same play. I knew Luke was going to throw the ball to me. I ran the same route and experienced the same outcome—I was wide open again. I couldn't shake the mental image of my earlier drop, though. This negative mental imagery and fear blocked my ability to make the play. I dropped the ball again!

Two wasted touchdown opportunities, I said to myself. *What's wrong with me?*

You might think two dropped passes is bad, but it got worse. It happened again. Same play. Same outcome. I dropped a THIRD deep pass!

HAVE YOU EVER FELT THAT WAY—WHEN IT JUST WASN'T YOUR DAY? DID YOU LET THIS FAILURE AFFECT YOUR PERFORMANCE THE REST OF THE SEASON?

That experience shook my confidence as a receiver, especially going on deep pass patterns. When fall came and the season began, I had the wrong mental approach. I was rattled. Instead of using mental imagery to replay past suc-

187

cesses and envision best-case scenarios, I would replay that day of drops, and I would try to avoid making the same mistake. *I was thinking below the line.* Though I increased my number of catches that season from the previous year, my average yards per catch decreased significantly. Due to my fear of dropping a deep pass, I would subconsciously keep my routes shorter.

For example, with a corner route, normally I would take a high angle toward the end zone, but because of my fear, I would bend down my angle to keep a flatter or more shallow angle.

This mindset took my average yards per catch from seventeen yards the year before to eleven yards that season.

Going into my senior year, I knew this mindset had to change. If I was going to play as my best self, I had to be a deep threat. I had to go for it. So, the night before our first practice in August, I sat down at my desk in my room, grabbed a piece of paper, and wrote down some goals. I wrote down that I wanted to lead the league in receiving; I wanted to earn all-state honors; I wanted to help lead our team to the state playoffs; and I wanted to earn a Division I scholarship.

I added two more words to this list. At the bottom of the page, I wrote in big letters GO DEEP. I knew that if I wanted to achieve my goals, I needed to fight through my fear of dropping a deep pass. I taped this piece of paper above my closet and looked at it every day before I went to school.

That phrase, "GO DEEP," was my personal mantra for that season. When my fear of failure (dropping a deep pass) would pop into my head like the year before, I would say to myself, *GO DEEP,* to help get my mind back on track and overcome my fear.

This strategy proved beneficial. My average yards per catch increased to twenty-two yards-per-grab that season. That is double than the year before! This improved mindset and production help me achieve my goals. I led the league in receiving and was the league offensive MVP. Despite having a new head coach and losing several key players from the year before, we won our league and went to the state play-offs. I earned all-state honors and hit my number one goal: I earned and accepted a full-ride scholarship offer to play in a major Division I conference.

CAN YOU COME UP WITH YOUR OWN PERSONAL RESET WORD OR MANTRA (LIKE MY "GO DEEP" EXAMPLE) THAT WILL HELP YOU ATTACK FEAR AND DRIVE YOU TO TAKE ACTION?

This contrast of two mental approaches (my negative junior year versus my positive senior year) is an example of the power of what I call "feeding the good wolf." This chapter is all about giving you the tools to feed your brain with productive thoughts, actions, knowledge, and wisdom from others.

Bad Wolf Versus Good Wolf
I mentioned this parable in my book *Project Rise*, and I want to revisit this concept, but in more detail.

An old Cherokee chief was teaching his grandson about life.

"A fight is going on inside me," he said to the boy. "It is a terrible fight, and it is between two wolves."

"One is evil—he is anger, envy, sorrow, regret, greed, ar-rogance, self-pity, guilt, resentment, inferiority, lies, false pride, superiority, self-doubt, and ego.

"The other is good—he is joy, peace, love, hope, serenity, humility, kindness, benevolence, empathy, generosity, truth, compassion, and faith.

"This same fight is going on inside you and inside every other person, too."

The grandson thought about it for a minute and then asked his grandfather, "Which wolf will win?"

The old chief simply replied, "The one you feed."

Like my example from my junior high school season, I was feeding the bad wolf by replaying past failures and by having a "don't do" mindset, instead of a "do" mindset.

So, how do you drive out darkness?

With light.

In this clash of good versus evil, the good wolf represents confidence, love, gratitude, and belief.

By feeding your spirit with gratitude and service, while feeding your mind through mentorship and investing in your personal development, you acquire the mental tools, proven strategies, and techniques to "feed the good wolf."

Feed Your Spirit
I love the David Guetta song featuring Justin Bieber called "2U." It has a rhythm and sound that makes me want to move—especially when the beat drops during the chorus. When doing mental conditioning training with groups, I'll sometimes use this song as an icebreaker to get people out of their seat, disrupt their normal classroom routine,

and move their bodies to change their physical and mental state. Some people are reluctant to dance because of embarrassment and insecurities of how they look. This is a perfect time for me to introduce the concept of performance anxiety.

The reason why I pick the song "2U" is because I explain that there are two yous. You are made up of what I call "B1" and "B2." B1 is your brain and B2 is your body. Sometimes your brain sabotages your body with an inner-critic and judge that hinders your performance (like an increased heart rate and breathing or juggling many nervous thoughts at once). Also, your body can sometimes sabotage your brain. Injuries occur (as we age our bodies break down and do not recover as well) and because we are human, we sometimes just flat-out make mistakes (drop a pass, make an error, miss a shot).

The goal is to quiet your brain and not let it get in the way of just letting your body do what it can naturally and normally do without critiquing every action. The ultimate goal, though, is to play in your spirit. There may be two yous, but we all have one spirit. Your spirit doesn't age, it doesn't have judgment, and when you play within your spirit, you are being your true authentic self, and in a state of flow.

I'm going to give you two ways to help feed your spirit, which will help lower stress and feed the good wolf. These two approaches are all about living with gratitude and serving others. Both are antidotes to stress and anxiety.

Gratitude
Do you know what the word "paradox" means? The *Merriam-Webster Online Dictionary* defines paradox as "one (such as a person, situation, or action) having seemingly contradictory qualities or phases."

Basically, a paradox is composed of two opposite forces coming together at once. Most athletes are in a state of paradox with their athletic careers. For example, let's say you just finished high school and have four years left to play in college. If you live to be a one hundred years old, that's only 4 percent of your life. Though your time competing as a student-athlete is brief, you have the vast majority of your life (about 80 percent) left to live once your career is over.

Can you see the paradoxical state here?

I remind many of the teams I work with that their time as athletes is fleeting, but their time alive post-career is vast. Thus, they must make it count. Living a life of regret because you didn't put in the work when you had opportunities is no way to live. It's vital to seize the moment and capitalize on this opportunity. Do not waste a single day. Many retired and former athletes I meet spend years reflecting on what they should have done or what they would have done differently back when they were playing. Many of these individuals wish they would have worked harder, practiced more, and spent more time in the weight room. Don't let this be you! This is what I call "Uncle Rico Syndrome" (for a good laugh, look up Uncle Rico from the movie *Napoleon Dynamite*).

ARE YOU MAXIMIZING EACH DAY WITH YOUR EFFORT AND COMMITMENT? DO YOU WAKE UP EACH DAY WITH A SENSE OF GRATITUDE?

During the relatively short time athletes have to compete in their prime, I suggest the way to make it count is taking nothing for granted and practicing the life-changing habit of gratitude.

Here is the challenge: **Exchange expectation with appreciation.**

While discussing the life-changing impact of gratitude with a group of high school softball players, a few of them did not know what the term gratitude meant. That's where Siri on my iPhone came in handy. Together, we asked the phone for the definition of gratitude and it said: "The quality of being thankful; readiness to show appreciation for and to return kindness." Thank you, Siri.

One of the reasons I preach the power of gratitude is because of the emotion of thankfulness. Being thankful is the antidote to worry and fear. When you choose to see the good and focus on what you have instead of what you don't have, you attract more positivity in your life. You become less anxious and reduce the stress hormone in your body called cortisol. During fight or flight moments and when stress is released, cortisol and adrenaline spike for our own survival from danger. Using deep, consistent breathing and focusing on gratitude has been shown to lower these stress levels.

DO YOU HAVE A GRATITUDE RITUAL?

Gratitude is a choice, and the act of thankfulness takes practice...just like practicing your free-throw shot. You cannot just practice it once and expect to improve. When you consistently practice gratitude, you create more of an optimist mindset. Optimism has the power to help you persevere through challenges and adversity at a greater level.

Martial arts legend Bruce Lee once said, "You have choice, you are the master of your attitude. Chose the positive, the constructive. Optimism is a faith that leads to success."

As I reflect on my career, I lacked a gratitude practice—mainly because I wasn't exposed to this powerful emotion. I heard plenty of lessons on how to be tough, compete, and give maximum effort, but most coaches did not, and still do not, have the word *gratitude* in their coaching playbook (if you are a coach reading this, it's time to add gratitude to your team's culture and language). Therefore, my anxiety and bouts with fear of failure hindered my ability to perform at my best.

Learn from my experience and research in positive psychology—gratitude is a flat-out game-changer. Below are a few ways to make gratitude a winning habit for you daily:

- Before you get out of bed each morning, take an inventory of all the things you are grateful for (your health, family, friends, teammates, mentors, and coaches). Let this prime your spirit to alter your mood to a positive one. Positivity and gratitude attract happiness. Happiness attracts more positive outcomes.
- Before each practice, game or match, take a one-minute gratitude moment. Soak it in. Use some self-talk to truly appreciate the opportunity to play and compete. Take a look around the field, court, or course. Don't just think about gratitude, but feel gratitude. This exercise will help lower some of the natural stresses of competition, help you relish the moment, and not take the opportunity in front of you for granted.
- Even in failure and hardship, find the lesson or something good that can come from that adversity. When you can find gratitude even in setbacks, your resiliency and ability to shorten the time to recover from failure will drastically improve.
- Start a Gratitude Journal. At the end of each day, write down small wins, moments that made you smile, les-

sons learned, and opportunities you are excited about.

GRATITUDE PRACTICE: TAKE A MOMENT AND WRITE DOWN AS MANY THINGS AS YOU CAN THINK OF THAT YOU ARE GRATEFUL FOR. REFER TO THIS LIST CONSISTENTLY AND ESPECIALLY BEFORE COMPETITION.

Service

How can you spot the alpha wolf in a pack of wolves? Is he in the front, middle, or back of the pack?

The alpha and leader of this group is always found in the back, watching over and protecting the pack. The point is... true leadership comes from a place of service.

In today's era—filled with SportsCenter highlights, re-Tweets, YouTube videos, and Instagram followers—I believe we are at an all-time high of narcissism, in which the focus is all about "me." This mindset of going out "to get mine," actually adds stress. When your focus is all about you and not about the team, you will not go as far, nor will you perform at your best. When we are struggling, our focus is usually all about "me." If this is you, try playing with a more team-first approach. Allow your teammates to share the burden of the spotlight. Here's the deal: No one is focusing solely on you anyway.

Here is an example to illustrate my point on the power of service and teamwork.

Have you ever seen a draft horse before? If you have, you know that it is a huge creature, much larger than a normal horse. Draft horses were used to farm, carry, and haul heavy objects before bulldozers, plows, and cranes were

195

ever invented. From the industrial revolution, to the invention of steel, railroads, and simply creating homes and buildings, draft horses were essential to our building and development of large structures.

Did you know that one draft horse can haul 8,000 pounds? So, let's test your math skills...how many pounds could two draft horses carry? If you answered 16,000 pounds, you are wrong. Two draft horses can haul 24,000 pounds working together. But wait! If a pair of draft horses spend a significant amount of time as a pair and learn to work together, they can haul a whopping 36,000 pounds. The most powerful pair of draft horses on record was able to pull an astonishing 100,000 pounds!

When you learn to serve your teammates and work together, you create a synergistic effect, meaning you help raise the level of production for not only yourself, but others also.

DO YOU GIVE OR TAKE ENERGY FROM OTHERS? DO PEOPLE LIGHT UP WHEN YOU **ENTER** OR **LEAVE** THE ROOM?

A benefit of unselfishness and serving others is the release of serotonin and dopamine in the brain. When you help someone, volunteer, give a compliment, or sacrifice for another, you are actually helping both your physical and mental health. Helping others has been proven to reduce stress, lower blood pressure, and actually lengthen life.

No one should win or worry alone. What are you doing to serve others? A way to better access a flow state is to work together with others toward a common goal. Make it a point to put your ego aside and be a servant leader. Because in the end, the only effective form of leadership is servant leadership.

Learn from one of the leading college football coaches of all time, former Pacific Lutheran University's national championship coach, Frosty Westering, and "make the big time where you are." The big time isn't a destination, but a place in your heart. According to the late Westering, a surefire way to reach the big time is to do your best at whatever role you play, and most importantly, serve others.

Be a clutch performer and serve someone today...because we rise by serving others.

HOW CAN YOU CAN YOU BETTER SERVE:
- YOUR FAMILY?
- YOUR FRIENDS?
- YOUR TEAMMATES?
- STRANGERS?

Make it a habit to do a random act of kindness each day. This tactic will help feed not only your spirit, but someone else's also.

Feed Your Mind
There are many stimuli vying for our attention: text messages, SnapChat, television, Netflix, friends, etc. What we do with our time, what we watch, listen to, read, and who we talk to, play a huge part in what shapes not only how we think but how we act. I find there are two effective ways to feed your mind with productive and positive information: through mentors and by investing in your personal development.

Mentorship
Are you a fan of *Star Wars?* I am. One of the many reasons why I love this science fiction franchise is because it introduced me to one of the greatest mentors in the history of the galaxy (and movie history), Jedi Master Yoda. This three-foot green Jedi said it well, "Always two there are. No more. No less. A master and an apprentice."

Whether in movies or real life, mentorship has been around for centuries as a way to expedite and advance learning. Plumbers, electricians, and doctors are just a few professional examples who value the importance of apprenticeship. And of course sports exemplifies the power of mentorship.

When the San Antonio Spurs selected Wake Forest University all-American center Tim Duncan in the first round of the 1997 NBA draft, the adjustment to living independently and playing at the highest level of basketball was a lot to handle.

Most number one overall draft picks do not play in NBA summer league games. Duncan, however, made the decision to play so he could improve his skills and adjust his game to the physical style of the NBA. Things did not go well that summer. Duncan's play was inconsistent, and he failed to experience the same type of dominance as college.

Luckily for this five-time NBA champion, fifteen-time all-star, and future Hall of Famer, he had a mentor—none other than the Spurs legend, Naval Academy graduate, and original member of the 1992 Olympic Dream Team, David Robinson.

At the time, Robinson had a family home in Colorado and invited Duncan to spend time and train there together before the season started. This training and mentorship paid

198

off. With a few mental and physical tweaks, Duncan applied learnings from Robinson, and he later earned NBA Rookie of the Year and All-NBA First-Team honors. By working together, Robinson and Duncan (called the "Twin Towers") later won two NBA championships together.

Like this example of Duncan and Robinson, mentorship helps you "draft" behind someone who has already been there and done that. The concept of drafting is utilized in sports in car and bike racing. When one drafts, he or she is racing directly behind another racer to conserve energy and effort. In this situation, the lead driver (Robinson) had already paved the way for the individual who was behind the lead rider (Duncan). Learn from this proven strategy.

Success leaves clues. Why should you try to reinvent the wheel? Study other dominant performers and their habits. Emulate the rituals that you think can help you (like the young Duncan did with the veteran Robinson). If possible, pick a successful athlete's brain and ask how he or she trains, prepares, deals with competition, stress, recovery, and handles off-the-field or court endeavors. Research suggests that though mentor insights improve performance, one of the biggest advantages comes from raising expectations. Mentorship has been shown to increase the standards of the individual being mentored. Ever heard of the saying, "Game recognizes game?"

By being around and emulating someone with more talent and experience than you, you will naturally raise your game. It's been said that you are a byproduct of the people you hang out with the most. Thus, it's time to be selective with who is in your inner-circle...including being intentional with selecting mentors.

The sky is the limit for what you can ask and learn. I've seen this strategy work for me in my own life. I assign myself new mentors every year in business, mental train-ing, and life. I would not be where I am today without this game-changing strategy.

WHO ON YOUR TEAM, IN YOUR NETWORK, OR EXPERT IN YOUR FIELD, CAN YOU ASK TO BE YOUR MENTOR? MAKE IT A POINT TO CHECK WITH THEM REGULARLY TO GAIN ESSENTIAL KNOWLEDGE TO REACH YOUR GOALS AND EXCEED YOUR POTENTIAL.

You can also select mentors that you can learn from by reading about them, watching their YouTube videos, and researching them online.

Humble yourself. Do not be too proud to learn from some-one else. If it worked for the two-time MVP Tim Duncan—and countless others ranging from all-stars, to all-Ameri-cans, and even billionaires—I know mentorship can work for you.

Personal Development
Do you have an absolute truth? When I say absolute truth, I mean something that you believe in with all your heart and soul to be true. I have a few absolute truths, but at the top of my list (besides my faith) is investing in my personal development. I believe that knowledge is power. The more I invest in my education, skill, experience, and brain power, the higher I go. Period.

There were many years as an athlete and business profes-sional where I simply got by on my talent and did not seek to learn everything I could in my field. As I reflect on those tough years, I felt like I was treading through sand, just trying to get by. There was even a point in my professional career when I hit such a stressful low point that I needed medication to lower my blood pressure. At that moment, while facing many sleepless nights, unfulfillment at work, and lack of engagement with my loved ones, I knew something needed to change.

That was precisely when I turned to knowledge.

The first book I read on the power of the mind was called *Positive Intelligence,* by Shirzad Chamine. I immediately saw improvement in my mental awareness and craved more. I later switched companies and met a veteran sales professional named Frankie Pretzel. Pretzel was a top performer every single year. He also happened to be a believer in the power of the brain, thought, and a winning mindset. He gave me a list of thirty books to read and/or listen to. This list changed my life and opened my mind to new strategies, proven techniques, and tools to implement winning habits.

If you think you can just show up and rely on your talent, you will begin to notice that other people (possibly less talented than you) will begin to pass you by. Remember: Your body has limits, but your mind is limitless.

WHAT ARE YOU DOING TO ENHANCE YOUR MENTAL DEVELOPMENT?

Here are a few examples on how you can fill your brain with positive information and knowledge:
- Books
- Audiobooks
- Podcasts
- YouTube videos
- Seminars and/or conventions

201

- Mentors
- Coaches
- Studying film
- Reviewing scouting reports

OF THESE EXAMPLES ABOVE, WHICH ONES CAN YOU UTILIZE MORE TO IMPROVE YOUR GAME?

I'll close this section with a story on the power of investing in your mental development, having a plan, and implementing it.

It was game one of the 1988 World Series. The Los Angeles Dodgers were playing the high-powered and heavily favored Oakland Athletics, led by American League MVP, Jose Canseco, and record-setting power hitter, Mark McGuire.

On this warm fall night in Los Angeles, as the Dodgers entered the bottom of the ninth inning down by one run, all the fans were up on their feet hoping for a miracle. The Dodgers had a tough challenge in front of them, though. They were facing the most dominant closer of that era, Dennis Eckersley. Normally, when "Eck" came into pitch, most considered the game over. He led the Majors in saves that year with forty-five.

With one runner on base and two outs, Dodgers Manager Tommy Lasorda made a bold move, he decided to pinch hit, and give veteran Kirk Gibson an opportunity of a lifetime. Without having had an at-bat all series, and not being fully healthy (Gibson had an injured hamstring on one leg and a bad knee on the other), many thought this was quite the gamble. Gibson, however, had been doing his homework on the A's pitching staff and was ready if his name was called.

This was a moment that a kid dreams of—a chance to be a hero on the biggest stage.

Despite getting behind in the count with zero balls and two strikes, Gibson (who won the 1988 National League MVP) worked the at-bat to a full count—three balls and two strikes. While taking a step out of the batter's box, he took a breath and remembered his pre-game scouting report from scout Mel Didier on Eckersley. Because Gibson spent time with his mental preparation and knowledge, he was confident he knew which pitch was coming next.

During a full count against lefties, Eck loves to throw his backdoor slider, Gibson remembered from his preparation.

With this knowledge, Gibson stepped back in the box with a plan: *Stay back, and sit on the slider.* While the Dodgers faithful and the world watched, this two time all-star, who could barely run, cracked one of the most famous home runs in the history of baseball. He did it. He came through in the clutch. With a giant grin, while the ball sailed over the right field wall, Gibson limped around the bases pumping his fist with heroic flair. His teammates rushed the field in celebration, and the crowd cheered and screamed with excitement.

While not having another plate appearance in the World Series, Gibson made his one opportunity count. The Dodgers later went on to defeat the A's in the World Series, 4-1.

This monumental clutch moment would not have happened if Gibson didn't take time to invest in his knowledge on the game, his opponent, and his plan.

This story reminds me of a phrase I learned while working with a professional baseball player recently. The quote that he loves to say is, "Plan the work, work the plan."

203

WHAT ARE YOU DOING TO DEVELOP YOUR PLAN? ARE YOU WAST-
ING THE DAY AND FILLING YOUR BRAIN WITH GARBAGE, OR WITH
PRODUCTIVITE INFORMATION TO IMPROVE YOUR EXECUTION?

Develop new knowledge and mental skills by investing in
your personal development daily. Then create a plan, and
implement it. If you apply this strategy, you just might be a
late game hero like Kirk Gibson.

Build and Trust Your Instincts
Help your body do what it is designed to do. Allow your mind
and spirit to connect with trust and without judgment. If a
player that I'm working with is struggling by being overly
critical or technical, I'll pull up YouTube and show him or
her a video from *National Geographic.* Do you think a cheetah worries about what the giraffe thinks of his running
technique, or what the birds flying above say about how he
attacks a herd of gazelles? Nope. Do you think the cheetah
overanalyzes his pouncing angle and shoulder motion? No
way. Nature is such a great teacher of peak performance.
The cheetah stays focused on his goal and lets his training
(which came from a parent), lessons from mistakes, and
natural instincts take over.

Your body is an amazing instrument. Get out of your own
way and enhance your instincts and focus by utilizing the
power of gratitude and service. Take your game to the next
level by learning from other successful individuals in your
field and attack learning with the same intensity as having healthy nutrition and training plans. What you put in
your brain is just as important as what you put in your
body. Invest in your personal development and call on that
knowledge when it is time to deliver.

204

Use these tactics to help harness the power of flow.

GLEASON

What would you do if you were seriously injured, diagnosed with cancer, or received news that slowly over time, you won't be able to walk and talk again? In 2011, my former teammate Steve Gleason received the harsh news that he was diagnosed with ALS (also known as Lou Gehrig's disease). Gleason is one of the most mentally tough individuals I have ever known. Upon learning his diagnosis, he filmed his journey, which was later made into a movie called *Gleason*.

WHAT WOULD YOUR OUTLOOK BE IF YOU HAD TO BE CONFINED TO A WHEELCHAIR FOR THE REST OF YOUR LIFE?

This is Steve Gleason's reality, but he hasn't given up, and I know he never will.

After watching Gleason's powerful documentary, I was so deeply touched that I wrote him a letter. By sharing this letter, I hope it gives you a new perspective on how truly blessed you are. Maybe the stress you feel as a performer might not feel as bad when you learn and hear stories of other people who are in challenging conditions. Gleason's story sure did that for me.

Dear Steve,

I have to make a confession. I've put off watching your award-winning film Gleason for months. When I learned you were diagnosed with ALS, I was shocked and deeply concerned for you and those close to you. I can't image what you and your family must have felt, but the news hit me hard. Almost as hard as the time you blindsided me during blitz pick-up my freshman year. You probably don't remember this, but I was lined up in the left slot. You were playing weak side linebacker on the far hash. I had the hot route over the middle, and just after Birny threw me the ball and the pigskin hit my hands, you ear-holed me and absolutely blew me up. I was five feet horizontal in the air because you hit me so hard. I somehow miraculously still held onto the ball and popped back up real quick to show that I was tough. No one seemed to care that this was a non-contact drill—maybe because I was a true freshman and you were a fifth-year senior.

Either way, I learned first hand what the term to get your "bell rung" meant. My left ear was ringing for like two hours after that play.

That hit obviously wasn't as hard as the adversities that you and your family face every day. As you say, "Awesome ain't easy," but I haven't been an awesome teammate. I've put off watching your honest and courageous journey that you documented in your movie for too long.

You see, you were like Superman to me—you still are, probably more so—and I cowardly didn't have the courage to witness your transformation...until last night. I balled my eyes out the entire film. I even went up to each of my chil-

dren and put my hands on them, while I was sobbing.

Like I did after you blindsided me, you keep getting back up every single day. You've refreshed my lens on life, like you undoubtedly have with millions of others.

I'm writing this right now because I can't sleep. You and your wife Michel's bravery is both haunting and heroic. I have to get a few things off my chest and share my feelings with you.

You probably haven't thought about me for a long time, but you've been on my mind for the past six years. The last time I saw you was late November 2011—just ten months after your diagnosis with ALS. I heard you were going to be honored in Pullman that weekend to raise the flag as an honorary captain.

There was an event for you at the Palouse Ridge Golf Course that Saturday, and I knew I had to see you. I've never told you this Steve, but I've always looked up to you. While I was a naive, wide-eyed, and insecure freshman, you were the confident big man on campus, senior captain. But what I've always loved about you is you've never acted like the big man on campus. You have always been so kind, full of energy, and open to talk to anyone—even me.

Though you made me sing the Cougar fight song in front of the entire team at the Cougar Fitness Buffet during fall camp, I didn't hold it against you. You made up for it when you came back to train with us in Pullman after your first year bouncing around the NFL as an undrafted free agent. You were learning to play safety, and I was a slot receiver. We had some good battles that summer. You gave many awesome insights about what it's like to be a professional to not only to me, but many other Cougar players who looked up to you, as well.

209

So back to your Cougar event in 2011—I remember seeing you walk through the venue door. You had a cane and something else unexpected. When I saw you I remember thinking, Holy crap, Steve's got a legit mustache. It was No-Shave November. You've always had the perfect combination of empathy, intensity, and a sense of humor.

Maybe it was fate or luck, but because I was standing closest to the door, I was the first person to hug you. After not seeing you for many years it touched me when you said, "Come in for the real thing." We hugged, and I felt so much love from you and everyone in that room. I've always felt some strange connection to you. Maybe it was because I felt we had a lot in common:

- *You went to Gonzaga Prep during the same time as my cousins Sarah and Peter Hession.*
- *We both were somewhat undersized as football players who didn't have that typical build or personality.*
- *Both of our fathers loved us, but in an intense, driven way.*
- *We both were two-sport athletes who played football and baseball.*

I remember several conversations we had about how you juggled both sports. These mini-mentor sessions really helped my mindset and confidence...if you could do it, I could do it too.

I'll never forget the speech you gave to the team during early August two-a-days, though. It was a hot summer Palouse evening and we were up in the Martin Stadium bleachers. Each week, one of the captains addressed the team with a speech. I've never forgotten your message. The topic of your talk was to DREAM BIG.

This mantra has carried you through your entire life. Watching from afar, you have lived this creed to its fullest—as an athlete, husband, father, son, friend, trailblazer, ALS advocate, filmmaker, role model, and a true inspiration.

Your Monday Night Football blocked punt may have been the symbol of rebirth to so many in New Orleans, but your will, grit, vulnerability, and vision living through ALS has given a rebirth to millions. You can add my name to that list.

Thank you for teaching me and others to fight through the fear and to dream big. Thank you for modeling raw vulnerability. Thank you for putting your family first (your wife Michel is one serious badass—we also share that in common, we married up!). And thank you for never giving up.

As I write this, the date is ironically 7/3, the opposite of your Saint's number, 37. Even though your life has played out the opposite of what you've envisioned, just know that your legacy in this world and impact on the development of ALS technology is making a larger imprint than you could have ever done as a player.

I see you now more powerful than Superman. You are like Obi-Wan Kenobi in Star Wars when he faced Darth Vader in that epic final battle where he said, "Strike me down, and I shall become more powerful than you can possibly imagine."

By sitting down in a chair Steve, you are helping me and others stand up—in relationships, life, and love.

All the best to Michel and Rivers. Tell your mom I said hello...she is one of the nicest people I've ever met, and I love seeing her when I go back to Pullman.

Congrats on your beautiful film Gleason. It is a must-see for

211

everyone.

Until next time I see you Steve, just know that I love you, and make sure that your head is on a swivel. I just might return the favor and blindside you with an ear-hole shot of my own—I don't care if you're in a wheelchair.

Either way, as always: Go Cougs, and No White Flags.

Sincerely, Your Friend and Teammate,
Collin

213

CHAPTER 8

RECOVERY

GRIND + REST = SUCCESS

During the summer of my junior football season in college, I had to add one more class to fulfill my credit requirement to earn my monthly scholarship check. While looking through the options, I noticed a Thursday afternoon yoga class. I had never taken yoga before and thought it would be a good experience to try something new and outside of my comfort zone. I recruited my roommate, "Mississippi Mark," and quarterback, Jason Gesser, to join me in this initial experience of zen.

Every Thursday afternoon for eight weeks spanning the months of June and July the three of us would head to the WSU student rec center to get our yoga on. This class was hosted by a sweet instructor, probably in her fifties, with a slim build, short graying haircut, soft comforting voice, and deep passion for sharing the benefits of yoga.

Yoga was a new experience that exposed me to many wonderful human performance concepts: learning the power of breath, connecting the mind and body, and practicing a form of meditation at the end of each class. By far, my favorite exercise was at the end of class. I can still see and feel myself lying peacefully on my back on top of my yoga mat. For ten to fifteen minutes, our instructor would guide us through a rejuvenating mindfulness session. This was the first time in my life that I was coached on how to breathe, relax, and simply focus on my breath and quiet my thoughts. No film, no lifting weights, no intense route-running, no homework, just me connecting to an energy from within.

Sometimes I would fall asleep during these relaxing moments. When we were asked to finally come back from our own little world, I remember feeling different. It was almost as if my brain just took a bath. I felt calm, clear, and a deep sense of rest. After yoga class, the three of us would leave the rec center and walk two blocks past the baseball and track fields to Martin Stadium. Two to three times a week during these summer months we would partake in player-led practices, including seven-on-seven scrimmages. Reflecting on that summer, Thursdays were always my best days. After yoga class, my body was refreshed, my mind was more focused, and my spirit was primed for competition. I did not fear failure, was less judgmental on outcomes, and felt more connected to the present moment. To use athlete speak, I "balled out" after yoga.

At the time I really did not make the connection *(Yoga + Rest + Meditation = Improved Football Performance)* because this type of mindfulness practice was so new and different—especially in a football locker room. After the summer session was over, I did not continue taking yoga classes. I remember thinking about asking our yoga instructor if we could work something out so she could come teach a mini-class once a week for our team. But I didn't. Insecurities, sticking to my peer norms, and a lack of self-awareness kept me from continuing this energy-shifting practice.

I should have trusted my gut. Many professional teams today offer yoga instruction as part of their training programs for recovery and rejuvenation. As fall came and we got into the flow of the season, my role was not as impactful as I envisioned. To cope with my lack of offensive involvement, I decided to work extra hard...including running extra pass patterns with our back-up quarterback, Chris Hurd.

Instead of helping, this extra grind actually hindered my performance. After two weeks of beating up my body after practice, Coach Mike Price called me into his office.

"Collin, I've noticed you've been taking extra reps after practice with Chris," he said. "I love the effort, but you've been looking slower on film. I think you should try resting, instead of going so hard."

Wow. My head coach now thinks I'm getting slower. My plan backfired, I thought.

Justin Su'a, Mental Conditioning Coach for the Boston Red Sox, says, "More isn't always better. Better is better." Like my examples above showed, Grind + Rest = Success. If you neglect the *rest* portion of this equation, your play will suffer. This chapter is all about helping you look at rest and recovery as a tool for peak performance. Your body is a fine-tuned machine. By maximizing your recovery, sleep, nutrition, and even nap habits, you'll be tapping into a natural performance enhancer.

I'm Tired
Many people do not actualize the power of sleep. According to the American Psychological Association, more than one-third (36 percent) of teens report feeling tired. And according to a study from YouGov.com, two-out-of-five adults (40 percent) are tired most of the week.

Seeing these alarming numbers, I make sure to incorporate a solid rest plan for the athletes I support with mental conditioning training. The data is just too strong to overlook this aspect of maximizing one's physical and cognitive potential. More sleep has been linked to improved reaction times, fewer mental errors, reduced injury rates, and longer playing careers.

Sara Mednick, PhD, a sleep researcher at the Salk Institute in La Jolla, California agrees: "Not only do athletes need sleep to improve on their athletic skills, but the restoration that occurs within muscles during deep sleep is important. If you don't get enough sleep it can be detrimental to your performance."

Stanford Snoozing

While conducting a mental function and sleep extension study on Stanford undergraduates, Cheri Mah, a researcher for the Stanford Sleep Disorders Clinic and Research Laboratory, had an aha moment. By chance, several of the participants in her study were on the swim team and recorded personal records during the periods of more sleep. She believed that more rest would improve cognitive aptitude, but her results in this initial study sparked a deep curiosity to explore the effects of sleep on physical performance, also.

With the help of sleep expert William Dement, MD, PhD, Mah studied eleven healthy Stanford basketball players for two basketball seasons. After recording baseline numbers, Mah found the players sleep ranged from six to nine hours per night. With her guidance, the participants increased this number by two hours per night during the season.

At the end of the sleep extension period, the players ran faster 282-foot sprints than they had at the beginning of the study—16.3 seconds versus 15.5 seconds. Their accuracy shooting the basketball improved, also. Their free throw percentages increased by 9 percent and three-point field goal percentages increased by 9.2 percent. Also, fatigue levels decreased following sleep extension, and the Stanford athletes reported improved performance in practices and games.

Mah, who now consults with the Golden State Warriors and other elite athletes, said regarding this research, "Additionally, our study suggests that significantly reducing an accumulated sleep debt from chronic sleep loss may require more than one night or weekend of recovery sleep. Although sleep is frequently overlooked and often the first to be sacrificed, sleep duration and sleep quality should be important daily considerations for athletes aiming to perform at their best."

This data really opened my eyes to the power of sleep, and I hope it does for you too. Let's explore in more detail what is happening to your body when you are catching a good night's snooze.

Five Stages of Sleep
One-third of our time on this earth is spent in bed. So what happens to our bodies and minds when we fall asleep? There are actually five stages that take place during this period of important rest. Below is a summary of the five sleep stages according to the *National Sleep Foundation* and the *Center for Sound Sleep:*

Stage 1 - Introduction to Sleep
In this early stage of sleep you are easily awakened. Your muscles begin to relax and your eyes move slowly back and forth and even twitch.

Stage 2 - Beginning of Sleep
This is the stage in which you spend about half of the night. In this stage, your body temperature drops, brain waves are slow, and your heart rate regulates. That means your heart and vascular system are getting a much needed rest, which might help to explain the many cardiovascular benefits of sleep recovery.

Stages 3 & 4 - Slow Wave Sleep

219

During stages three and four, which are the restorative stages of sleep (also known as "slow wave sleep"), blood pressure drops, breathing slows down, blood flow moves to the muscles, and tissue is repaired. Deep sleep is a natural performance enhancer, which is most evident in this stage. Hormones, such as the human growth hormone, are secreted at this time to help with recovery.

Stage 5 - Rapid Eye Movement (REM)
REM sleep dominates the latter half of the sleep period, especially the hours before waking, and accounts for up to 20 to 25 percent of total sleep time in adults. Muscles become completely paralyzed and unresponsive during REM sleep. The majority of dreams—certainly the most memorable and vivid dreams—occur during REM sleep.

For more information on how you can better maximize your sleep, check out these helpful resources:

- National Sleep Foundation: www.sleepfoundation.org
- The Center for Sound Sleep: www.centerforsoundsleep.com
- Download one of these top-four sleep phone apps, selected by *Medical News Today* (for iPhone and Android):
  » *Relaxing Melodies*
  » *Sleep Cycle*
  » *Recolor*
  » *Sleep Time*
- Utilize wrist wear to help you track and monitor your sleep:
  » *Apple Watch*
  » *Fitbit*

Body and Brain
Sleep doesn't just help our bodies recover and perform better, but it helps our brains, too. Philip Gehrman, PhD, assistant professor of psychiatry at the University of Penn-

sylvania, suggests that sleeping "seems to be related to forming the pathways in the brain for memory and learning." An additional study by Matthew A. Wilson, associate professor of brain and cognitive sciences in Massachusetts Institute of Technology's Picower Center for Learning and Memory, supports this. In this breakthrough study, Wilson found that rats' memories of a sequential experience, such as following a maze, were reactivated during REM sleep. The researchers monitored the firing activity of collections of neurons in each rat's hippocampus as the rat ran on a simple track for a food reward. Similar brain cells would fire during sleep. Meaning, the rats figured out ways to find cheese in the maze while they were catching some Zs.

My takeaway here: The fewer hours of sleep you get, the fewer opportunities your brain is allowed not only to recover, but possibly find solutions to achieve your goals also.

Tip: Before you go to bed at night, set an intention of what you would like your subconscious to help you uncover or figure out during your time asleep.

Naps
Currently, nearly half of Americans say that insufficient sleep affects their daily activities, according to research from the *National Sleep Foundation.* The implications extend beyond health. According to a September 2011 study from the *Journal of Sleep,* lack of sleep cost U.S. companies a staggering $63 billion in lost productivity.

Recognizing this problem, many companies like Google, the Huffington Post, Zappos, and even Uber endorse taking a light snooze during the day. Why is this? Research suggests that naps can improve brain functions ranging from memory, alertness, focus, production, and creativity. A power nap is a short sleep (twenty minutes or less), which ends prior to deep sleep (slow wave sleep), intended to quickly revitalize the napper. If you sleep too long (more than thirty minutes), it takes longer to get out of a state of drowsiness. Research from a 1995 NASA study showed that a twenty-six-minute nap enhanced performance by 34 percent and overall alertness by 54 percent. This data inspired the National Transportation Safety Board (NTSB) to suggest that air traffic controllers be allowed to take short naps during their workday in order to remain more alert while on the job.

All these facts and figures aside, I've experienced this heightened sense of alertness and creativity after a nap myself. I call the time just after waking up from a nap "nap residue." I often gain clarity on a problem, get a new idea, or find a solution during the moments coming out of a nap and just before being fully awake.

The inventor of the light bulb, Thomas Edison, would use naps as a tool to find creativity, while tinkering with new inventions. Edison was not the only one who utilized naps as a performance enhancer. Famous leaders such as John F. Kennedy, Ronald Reagan, Lyndon B. Johnson, Napoleon Bonaparte, and Winston Churchill used daily naps as part of their routine.

Churchill once said, "Nature has not intended mankind to work from eight in the morning until midnight without that refreshment of blessed oblivion which, even if it only lasts twenty minutes, is sufficient to renew all the vital forces."

What about athletes?

When Andy Murray won *Wimbledon* in 2013, he become the first Brit to do so in seventy-seven years. During that historic tournament, he was sleeping twelve hours per night. "Rest is so important," he told *The Mirror* (a news outlet in the U.K.). "On the days when I am not playing I try to get in and do my work early, deal with everything else that has to happen, and then get home and have a nap. I don't normally have any trouble sleeping. I sleep well. You need rest to make sure you recover properly."

Two-time NBA MVP and world champion, Stephen Curry, makes napping part of his game day routine. "When you wake up from a nap, you know what time it is, you know it's time to get ready and get focused and go to the game," he told the New York Times.

HOW CAN YOU INCORPORATE A SHORT NAP INTO YOUR REST AND RECOVERY PLAN?

Just remember that a short nap is usually recommended (about twenty minutes) while preparing for a practice or a game. This type of nap provides significant benefit for improved alertness and performance without leaving you feeling groggy or interfering with nighttime sleep. Longer naps can leave people with *sleep inertia,* especially when they last more than twenty or thirty minutes. Sleep inertia is the feeling of grogginess and disorientation that can come with awakening from a deep sleep. While this state usually lasts for a few minutes to a half-hour, it can be detrimental to those who must perform immediately after waking from a napping period.

Rest List
While working with a Major League Baseball player during the off-season, we discussed the power of recovery and rest. This high achiever was looking to obtain any edge possible. Based on the science and overwhelming evidence, we agreed that being more intentional about sleep and restful habits should be one of his top pillars of peak performance.

223

Here is the list we came up with to support his recovery plan, as well as some notes about each point:

- *Sleep:* He increased his eight hours of sleep average each night up to nine to eleven hours per night (this took extreme discipline!). That meant he stopped using his phone well before he went to bed. Also, he created consistent times of when he went to sleep and woke up in the morning.
- *Mindfulness Meditation:* He started using the Headspace app at least once a day. During these ten-minute guided meditation sessions, he practiced quieting his thoughts, resting his mind, and connecting with the present moment. (Headspace has a great series on competition...check it out).
- *Journaling:* To help him feel refreshed and reduce stress, he captured his thoughts, experiences, feelings of gratitude, and intentions in a journal (specifically, he used the *Rise Journal,* which is my published journaling book). This practice helped him gain perspective, introspection, and a sense of clarity.
- *Sensory Deprivation:* During one of our sessions, I introduced him to Restricted Environmental Stimulation Therapy (REST), also known as floating in a float tank. What is REST exactly? The person in a float tank (or pod) is suspended in a solution of warm water and Epsom salt without sound or light. This relaxation technique produces significant physical and mental benefits and creates a feeling of being weightless. He enjoyed the positive effects mentally and physically so much, he began to float once a week.
- *Naps:* He would mix in a ten- to twenty-five-minute nap most days—especially when he felt he did not reach his nightly sleep goal the night before.
- *Visualization:* He developed the daily routine of visualizating his objectives and best-case scenarios that he was striving for. By taking these mental reps, he was

able to use imagery to improve his preparation, while conserving physical energy.

- *Cold Shower:* He started finishing his showers with cold water. Cold temperatures are proven to reduce inflammation. These quick bursts of water fostered a more rapid rate of recovery for his muscles.
- *Cryotherapy:* Some call whole-body cryotherapy the ultimate cold shower. Though he did not perform this recovery technique while working with me, he planned on standing in a cryo-chamber during the season. Cryo consists of exposing the entire body to subzero temperatures, sometimes even below -200 degrees Fahrenheit, for a few minutes (typically between two and four minutes...anything longer would be dangerous). After performing cryotherapy, the body warms up through vasodilation, which fosters many health benefits including athletic recovery, muscle repair, reduction of chronic pain, and inflammation.
- *Fun Hobbies:* Sometimes, we just need a break. He wrote down his favorite activities away from the game to help him unplug and reload—especially on days off.

WRITE YOUR OWN REST LIST. USE THE EXAMPLES ABOVE TO CREATE A DETAILED RECOVERY PLAN TO HELP YOU RECHARGE YOUR BATTERIES, SO YOU CAN PERFORM AT YOUR BEST.

Energy Scale

While working with a softball player one day, I noticed she seemed very tired. I tried not to be offended by her constant yawning during one of our sessions. Halfway into our meeting, I asked her, "How much sleep are you getting per night?"

She said, "About six hours." I then asked her to rate on

a scale from one to ten how she felt (one being extremely exhausted, and ten being filled with endless energy). I call this the "Energy Scale."

"About a three," she said.

It made sense. Her schedule was as robust as any professional or amateur athlete I had ever seen. From going to class to homework to practice to individual lessons and strength training...she took having a full plate to a whole new level. We set a goal for her to get at least eight hours of sleep each night (which meant going to bed at 9:30 p.m.) and mixing in a ten- to twenty-minute nap during the day. I challenged her to perform this routine for the next seven days.

When we met back again the following week, she looked like a different person. Her score jumped from a three to an eight (that's five points!). She seemed very excited about this. By adding more than two hours of extra sleep and roughly fifteen minutes of napping each day, she was giving her body an extra fifteen hours and forty-five minutes of rest and recovery time for the week (that's sixty-three hours a month...or more than two-and-a-half extra days of recovery for the month). She reported that she had more energy, was less stressed, and was even more alert. She noticed an improvement in her performance not only in athletics, but in school also.

NOW IT'S YOUR TURN. USE THE ENERGY SCALE AND RATE YOUR ENERGY FROM ONE TO TEN.

LOW **1 2 3 4 5 6 7 8 9 10** HIGH

HOW CAN YOU MAKE REST AND RECOVERY A MAJOR FOCUS TO IMPROVE YOUR GAME?

Take the seven-day *Energy Scale Challenge.* Set some goals on what time you will go to bed, wake up, and take a power nap (no more than twenty minutes). Create a plan. This exercise will take discipline and sacrifice, but remember: Winners do what others are not willing to do.

Check back in after seven days and record your score on the *Energy Scale.* Evidence shows that you will be a better you if you invest in yourself and get more sleep. Rest is a key component of flow. If world class performers like athletes Maria Sharapova, LeBron James, Roger Federer, and Lindsey Vonn say that sleep is one of their secrets to success, it's time to add this strategy as part of your game plan, too.

Nutrition and Hydration
Though I don't specialize in nutrition, I certainly understand the importance of being well-fueled for competition versus working out or lacing up for a game without the proper nutritional foundation. To say you're starting on empty to begin with is an understatement. Just as sleep is

vitally important for your performance and recovery, so are nutrition and hydration.

You may have heard the phrase "energy in equals energy out," but no two athletes are created equal, and everyone has his or her unique nutritional needs, so it's difficult to generalize what athletes need daily. It's important to nourish your body with good foods rather than garbage. Small changes in your diet can lead to rewards such as increased energy and focus. Also, drinking enough water before, during, and after, as well as understanding the correct additional fluids for your body (not everyone needs sports drinks!) will benefit you just as the proper rest and recovery will.

If you wait until the night before or the day of the game to properly hydrate and eat nourishing foods, it could be too late. Proper nutrition—especially hydration—is a daily exercise. If you want to be a real baller, then trade the soda pop for what Adam Sandler's character in the movie, *The Waterboy,* calls "some high quality H2O."

Tip: Try writing down what you eat and drink every day for three days. It helps to write down the times you eat, also. Don't leave anything out and include your practice and/or game times in your list.

HOW DID YOU FEEL EACH OF THESE DAYS? DID YOU HAVE EXTRA ENERGY, A GREAT PERFORMANCE, OR DID YOU COME IN LAST PLACE DURING RUNNING DRILLS AT PRACTICE?

Your food and fluid intake could be affecting your performance. Ask your coach, mentor, or nutrition resource at school or for your team (if you have one) to assist in making sure you are fueling up properly to meet your performance goals.

To sum it up, utilize the power of sleep, rest, nutrition and hydration, and recovery. The beautiful thing about these areas is you have control over how much rest you give yourself and what you put into your body. If you take this part of your game seriously, you will help access a flow state and maintain a higher level of focus and energy.

MIND
MATTER

ERIC'S IMAGE

Eric was not doing very well. The high school junior was barely getting by with his grades. He hated school, and several of his teachers did not believe he would even graduate. While in class, Eric barely paid attention, and he would spend more time being the class clown than listening and doing his school work.

After seeing his first semester report card that junior year, Eric told his mom, "I'm just not very smart. I don't think that I'm cut out to go to college." He added, "The SATs are coming up, but what's the use of even taking them?"

Eric's mom was very supportive and encouraged her son to give the SAT a shot. "You have nothing to lose," she told him. "There may be some colleges you can get into, but you'll never know your capabilities if you do not at least take that test."

"OK, Mom, OK, I'll take the test," he said begrudgingly. The next day Eric signed up.

A month went by, and with no surprise, Eric hadn't studied at all. He showed up to take the SAT and felt that it was hard but that he did know some of the answers. There were many tough questions though, and he tried to cheat, but everyone's tests around him looked different than his. He did his best to at least write down an answer and not leave one blank. When Eric finished, he turned his test in with a sigh of relief and said, "I'm glad that's over."

Several months went by, and Eric's behavior started to get even worse. He went to detention for fighting after school, and he was failing his chemistry class. Eric's mom was stressed worrying about her boy when an envelope arrived in the mail. It was the results of his SAT test. After school that day they opened it together not expecting much.

Fearing the worst, they received an extreme surprise when they saw his score: 1500 (out of 1600). They both almost fainted. "What!," Eric's mother screamed. "A 1500! Is that right? Eric, did you cheat?"

"No, Mom, I didn't. I promise," Eric responded. "To be honest, I tried, but everyone's test was different. Maybe I am smart after all."

They couldn't believe it. Maybe Eric was intelligent but just wasn't focusing or trying hard in school. The test results really motivated Eric, and he began to make some changes. He stopped skipping class. He paid more attention during lectures, and for the first time in his life he was turning in all of his homework assignments on time. Eric really had a transformation. His mom was most excited about the fact that Eric stopped hanging out with certain individuals that were bringing him down with their behavior.

"Maybe college is for me," Eric told his mom.

With all of his hard work during his senior year in high school, Eric was able to get his GPA up to a level where he would graduate. His improved focus and commitment paid off. Upon graduation, Eric was accepted and attended a small four-year college about two hours north of his home.

He thrived in the college environment and eventually graduated with honors. Years later, Eric became the CEO of a popular magazine brand, and he credits receiving his high SAT score as the turning point of his life.

"My self-image really changed after taking that test," he often said. "For once in my life I actually believed in myself."

When visiting his mom with his wife and two children many years later for Christmas (sixteen years after he graduated from high school), Eric's mom had an envelope waiting for him. It was from the College Board and the Educational Testing Service (ETS), which developed the SAT. "Eric, this is for you," his mom said while sipping a cup of coffee. "This envelope arrived about two weeks ago."

While reading this letter standing around the kitchen island, the ETS informed Eric that there was a mistake on his test. While performing an internal audit, they found that in the past sixteen years, a handful of individuals were sent the wrong test results. They apologized, but his score was actually a 710—not a 1500.

"What? How can this be?" Eric asked his mom with astonishment.

"Who cares about this letter, dear?" His mom responded. "That mistake helped you find your true potential."

She was right. Even though Eric's grades and SAT results would suggest that his intelligence during high school was average or below average versus his peers, Eric turned his life around. By having a more positive self-image, his habits, actions, and behaviors changed.

233

This lesson, which is actually based on a true story, is that excellence is not fixed, but can grow...and it all starts with how you see yourself.

Earlier in this book, you learned how Andy the Elephant was not able to break his untrue negative self-image (a lack of strength). Eric's story is much different—he was able to break free from his internal chains.

HOW IS YOUR SELF-IMAGE?

It's time to believe in yourself, take control of your life, and begin to change key habits that will help lead you to success. You do not need a false test score, external validation, your past or current situation to begin your own journey of self-confidence. Decide today that you are enough and that you have everything you need to reach or exceed your potential.

The power of belief and self-image are the most powerful forces we have. Change your self-talk and your image will improve. Change your image, and your actions will match that image. With an improved self-image and actions, your results will shift. With better results, the stronger your belief will become.

You got this! I believe in you. Like Eric's story shows, the most important image is your own internal vision.

WHAT AREAS OF YOUR LIFE ARE YOU SELF-SABOTAGING WITH A NEGATIVE IMAGE OF YOURSELF?:

- SCHOLASTICS?
- ATHLETICS?
- SOCIAL?
- DATING?
- LEADERSHIP?
- YOUR FITNESS?
- TRYING NEW THINGS?
- CAREER OPPORTUNITIES?
- PUBLIC SPEAKING?
- BOUNCING BACK FROM FAILURE?
-

WHAT STEPS CAN YOU TAKE TO IMPROVE YOUR SELF-IMAGE?

Continue to use the principles from this book consistently. Rome was not built in a day, and neither will the best version of you. Identify your strengths. Focus on your vision. Stop comparing and obsessing what others think of you. Zero in on your values, and just be you. But more importantly, take the necessary actions needed to grow and improve...that is where ultimate fulfillment is found.

Make a change for the better. Commit. Believe. Work hard. Persist. And lastly, give yourself GRACE. If you follow this recipe, you will unlock your full potential...just like Eric.

CLOSING

BELIEVE

YOU CAN DO THIS

Several years ago, I was playing basketball with one of my mentors, Brett McDaniel (a.k.a. McD), in a local spring league game. McD was an amazing athlete and leader at Puyallup High School and later at Western Washington University as a standout football player. Being a few years older than me, McDaniel has always been someone that I have admired. He is kind, smart, hard-working, and passionate about making an impact in the lives of others.

With the sounds of basketballs bouncing and shoes squeaking on the gym floor, McD came up to me and invited me to come speak to his high school leadership class later that month. I responded with an enthusiastic, "Yes!" I was excited to share the personal growth that I had recently experienced. During that time, I had been consuming book after book on the power of the mind, and was learning how self-image, self-talk, and perception were closely tied to human performance. With this new awareness, my self-sabotaging inner voices were not as loud anymore. I was crushing my sales numbers at work and saw firsthand how having a winning mindset can be life-changing.

This invitation from McDaniel was a blessing because it forced me to come up with a personal philosophy and framework to teach and inspire others. I felt like I had something special and vital to share. I tailored my message to my younger self and wanted to teach the classroom

237

lessons not often taught in schools about courage, goals, habits, visualization, vulnerability, gratitude, service, and the power of our thoughts.

My time with these high school students was amazing. The experience of telling my story was invigorating and rewarding. I felt like I was really connecting with the students and that my message was resonating. A few hours after my talk, I received a phone call.

While I was going on a walk in my neighborhood, passing trees and blooming spring flowers, McDaniel called. I answered my iPhone and listened to him utter these life-changing words, "You can do this."

I responded somewhat dumbfounded with a curious, "Huh?"

Like the supportive mentor, coach, and father he is, McDaniel replied, "No, seriously. You can be a mental conditioning coach. There is a huge need for what you just shared."

McD, being a successful basketball coach and passionate researcher in positive psychology, gave me several names to look up of people relating to high-performance coaching, including Russell Wilson's and University of Alabama's football mental conditioning coach, Trevor Moawad. I had no idea that this was actually a career path. I thought that only PhD sports psychologists did this type of work.

I started researching the industry and found a plethora of college and professional organizations that utilize mental skills training from mental coaches such as Brian Cain, Justin Su'a, and Lindsey Wilson. My mind was blown. I was already teaching many of these principles as a sales trainer and coach. From that moment on, I committed myself to the field of high performance.

During this journey, I have had the pleasure of working with a variety of professional and ameture athletes, coaches, and teams. I have taught a wide range of sales professionals, leaders, and organizations as a sales trainer. I have spoken at elementary, middle school, high school, and college campuses on the power of our thoughts and habits. None of this would have been possible if Brett McDaniel did not call me to share his faith in me. His encouragement gave me the confidence in myself that *I can actually do this*. And here I am, several years later, actually making my dream a reality.

McD was that voice that kick-started my belief and path to follow my passion. Let the pages in this book and my words encourage you to do the same. YOU MUST BELIEVE! We only have one life to live. Follow these steps and you will be on your own journey of mastery:

1. Step outside your comfort zone, and answer this question: *What do I want?*
2. Based on your answer, create a plan of attack and develop your process.
3. Take consistent and deliberate action to execute your plan.
4. Monitor your self-talk, have balance, and believe with all of your heart that you can do this.
5. Measure your progress and adjust your approach if needed...never quit!

Use the principles in this book to win the most important game—the inner-game. The more you apply these tactics, strategies, and routines, the more you are likely to **unlock the power of flow.**

Be balanced...you are more than one thing.

239

Develop a process...repeated actions become instinct.

Have courage...get comfortable being uncomfortable.

Have vision...the most powerful force is how you see yourself.

Earn it...shape your habits or your habits shape you.

Advertise...master your self-talk and visualize what you want.

Feed the good wolf...invest in yourself and others and you will rise.

Recover...Grind + Rest = Success.

What do you have to lose? Are you afraid of failure? Remember, failure is feedback and part of the process. As football coach Nick Saban says, "Don't waste a mistake. Learn from it." The only way you can fail is if you give up.

Acclaimed New Zealand cricket player Mac Anderson once said, "Never underestimate the power of belief when it comes to fulfilling your dreams. I can say without hesitation that every person I've ever met who has achieved any degree of success has one thing in common: they believed with all their heart they could do it."

The power of belief is real.

I'll say it again: In order to master your mindset, win the inner-game, and unlock the power of flow...YOU HAVE TO BELIEVE!

Make today the day when you face your fears and go for it. Trust me, you will thank yourself years from now if you decide right now to make the necessary changes to master your mindset. That is the key, you must DECIDE. Burn the boats, don't look back, and commit to this approach.

You got this. I believe in you! It is time to quiet that in-ner-judge and believe in yourself. You only get one shot at life...make it count.

The body has limits...but the mind is limitless.

ACKNOWLEDGEMENTS

Thank you, Kendra, for supporting and encouraging me to follow my passion. I'm in a flow state every time I'm with you. You are my bliss.

To Baylor, Bellamy, Winnie, and Norah: My number one performance goal is to love and serve you every day. Being the best daddy is what drives me. You are my true north.

Thank you, Mom, Dad, Patrick, Tammy, Ray, and all of my family and friends who support me daily.

A huge thank you goes out to my mom, Susan Henderson, Eric Eagon, and most importantly, Kate Bethell, for doing an amazing job editing this book.

Trols, B-Mar, Eagon, and Jameel: Thanks for supporting me and my passion to teach the inner-game to student-athletes.

A big thank you goes out to the teams, athletes, coaches, students, managers, sales professionals, parents, individuals, and leaders that I have been blessed to work with. I have learned more from you than I could have ever taught you.

Finally, below is a list of my mental mentors in the field of high performance that have helped shape my philosophy and knowledge. To these positive psychology giants, thank you so much for your important work and guiding me in my own journey of peak performance. In no particular order:

- Dr. Mihaly Csikszentmihalyi
- Brett McDaniel
- Trevor Moawad
- Dr. Michael Gervais
- Justin Su'a
- Brian Cain
- Tony Robbins
- Dr. Bhrett McCabe
- Lindsey Wilson
- Ryan Dambach
- Dr. Colleen Hacker
- Lewis Howes
- Dr. Heidi Grant
- Dr. Ken Ravizza
- Steven Kotler
- Dr. Angela Duckworth
- Steve Magness
- Brad Stulberg
- Tim Ferriss
- Dr. Carol Dweck
- Dr. Brené Brown
- Dr. K. Anders Ericsson
- Brendon Burchard
- Jon Gordon

I encourage you to continue your own quest of winning the inner-game by researching these game-changers through their websites, social media sites, podcasts, books, and YouTube videos.

Win the inner-game...dominate the outer-game.

REFERENCES

SOURCES THAT SHAPED THIS BOOK

This book could not have been created without outstanding and informative work from other brilliant thinkers, researchers, and practitioners in the field of high performance. Below is a list of sources that I either cited directly, inspired my thought process, or helped me create my own philosophy and theories that I share in this book. Some stories and quotes featured in *Master Your Mindset* have been absorbed during lectures or in personal interviews throughout my career. I've made a tremendous effort to give credit where exceptional credit is due.

Books

Afremow, Jim. T*he Champion's Mind: How Great Athletes Think, Train, and Thrive.* New York: Rodale, 2013.

Anchor, Shawn. *The Happiness Advantage: How a Positive Brain Fuels Success in Work and Life.* New York: Crown Business, 2010.

Brown, Brené. *Daring Greatly: How the Courage to Be Vulnerable Transforms the Way We Live, Love, Parent, and Lead.* New York: Avery, 2012.

Cain, Brian. *Toilets, Bricks, Fish Hooks and PRIDE: The Peak Performance Toolbox Exposed.* Peak Performance Publishing, 2011.

Chamine, Shirzad. *Positive Intelligence: Why Only 20% of Teams and Individuals Achieve Their True Potential and How You Can Achieve Yours.* Austin: Greenleaf Book Group, 2012.

Csikszentmihalyi, Mihaly. *Flow and the Foundations of*

Positive Psychology: The Collected Works of Mihaly Csikszentmihalyi. Dordrecht: Springer, 2014.

Duhigg, Charles. *The Power of Habit: Why We Do What We Do in Life and Business.* New York: Random House, 2012.

Dweck, Carol. *Mindset: The New Psychology of Success.* New York: Ballantine, 2006.

Duckworth, Angela. *Grit: The Power of Passion and Perseverance.* New York: Scribner, 2016.

Fabritius, Friederike and Hans W. Hagemann. *The Leading Brain: Neuroscience Hacks to Work Smarter, Better, Happier.* New York: TarcherPerigee, 2017.

Gallwey, W. Timothy. *The Inner Game of Tennis: The Classic Guide to the Mental Side of Peak Performance.* New York: Random House Trade Paperbacks, 2008.

Gladwell, Malcolm. *Outliers: The Story of Success.* New York: Little, Brown and Company, 2008.

Jeter, Derek. *The Life You Imagine: Life Lessons for Achieving Your Dreams.* New York: Three Rivers Press, 2000.

Kotler, Steven. *The Rise of Superman: Decoding the Science of Ultimate Human Performance.* New York: Houghton Mifflin Harcourt, 2014.

Lentz, Carl. *Own the Moment.* New York: Simon & Schuster, 2017.

Mack, Gary and David Casstevens. *Mind Gym: An Athlete's Guide to Inner Excellence.* New York: McGraw-Hill, 2001.

Maltz, Maxwell. *Psycho-Cybernetics: Updated and Expanded.* New York: Perigee, 2015.

McCabe, Bhrett. *The Game Plan: Managing Your Champ & Chump.* 606 Publishing, 2018.

McCabe, Bhrett. *The MindSide Manifesto: The Urgency to Create a Competitive Mindset.* 606 Publishing, 2017.

McCormack, Mark. *What They Don't Teach You at Harvard Business School: Notes from a Street-Smart Executive.* New York: Bantam Books, 1984.

Meyer, Urban. *Above the Line: Lessons in Leadership and Life from a Championship Program.* New York: Penguin Books, 2015.

Post, Stephen G. *The Hidden Gifts of Helping: How the Power of Giving, Compassion, and Hope Can Get Us Through Hard Times.* San Francisco: Jossey-Bass, 2011.

Rankin, Lissa. *Mind Over Medicine: Scientific Proof That You Can Heal Yourself.* New York: Hay House, 2013.

Stulberg, Brad and Steve Magness. *Peak Performance: Elevate Your Game, Avoid Burnout, and Thrive with the New Science of Success.* New York: Rodale, 2017.

Su'a, Justin. *Parent Pep Talks: The Mental Skills Your Child Must Have to Succeed in School, Sports, and Life.* Springville: Plain Sight, 2013.

Veach, Chad. *Faith Forward Future: Moving Past Your Disappointments, Delays, and Destructive Thinking.* Nashville: Nelson Books, 2017.

Willink, Jocko. *Discipline Equals Freedom: Field Manual.* New York: St. Martin's Press, 2017.

Podcasts

Howes, Lewis. "Episode 420: Finish Strong." *The School of Greatness.* Podcast audio, January 7, 2018. https://lewishowes.com/podcast/finish-strong/

Ferriss, Tim. *The Tim Ferriss Show.* Podcast audio. https://tim.blog/podcast

Elrod, Hal. *Achieve Your Goals.* Podcast audio. http://halelrod.com/podcast

Su'a, Justin. *Increase Your Impact.* Podcast audio. http://increaseyourimpact.libsyn.com

Gervais, Michael. *Finding Mastery: Conversations with Michael Gervais.* Podcast audio. https://findingmastery.net/category/podcasts

Articles & Websites

Abrams, Jonathan. "Napping on Game Day is Prevalent Among NBA Players," *The New York Times.* March 6, 2011. http://www.nytimes.com/2011/03/07/sports/basketball/07naps.html.

Adams, AJ. "Seeing is Believing: The Power of Visualization,"*Psychology Today.* December 3, 2009. https://www.psychologytoday.com/us/blog/flourish/200912/Seeing-is-believing-the-power-visualization.

"Amazon.com Announces Third Quarter Sales up 34% to $43.7 Billion," *Business Wire.* October 26, 2017. https://www.businesswire.com/news/home/20171026006422/en/Amazon.com-Announces-Quarter-Sales-34-43.7-Billion.

Anxiety and Depression Association of America, https://adaa.org. *"Any Anxiety Disorder," National Institute of Mental Health.* November 1, 2017. https://www.nimh.nih.gov/health/statistics/any-anxiety-disorder.html.

Bethune, Sophie. *"American Psychological Association* Survey Shows Teen Stress Rivals That of Adults," American Psychological Association. February 11, 2014. http://www.apa.org/news/press/releases/2014/02/teen-stress.aspx.

Brandt, Michelle. "Snooze You Win? It's True for Achieving Hoop Dreams, Says Study," *Stanford Medicine.* June 30, 2011. https://med.stanford.edu/news/all-news/2011/07/snooze-you-win-its-true-for-achieving-hoop-dreams-says-study.html.

The Center for Sound Sleep, www.centerforsoundsleep.com.

Ellis, Ralph. "Wimbledon Men's Final: Andy Murray Reveals 12 Hours of Sleep a Day is His Secret to Success," *Daily Mirror.* July 6, 2013. https://www.mirror.co.uk/sport/tennis/Wimbledon-mens-final-andy-murray-2034019.

Ericsson, K. Anders, Ralf Th. Krampe, and Clemens Tesche-Romer. "The Role of Deliberate Practice in the Acquisition of Expert Performance." *New York Times*. 1993. http://www.nytimes.com/images/blogs/freakonomics/pdf/DeliberatePractice(PsychologicalReview).pdf.

Geoghegan, Tom. "Who, What, Why: How Long is the Ideal Nap?," *BBC News*. April 29, 2011. http://www.bbc.com/news/world-us-canada-13232034.

Goldman, Scott. "Mind, Body and Sport: Anxiety Disorders—An Excerpt from the Sport Science Institute's Guide to Understanding and Supporting Student-athlete Mental Wellness," *NCAA*. October 8, 2014. http://www.ncaa.org/sport-science-institute/mind-body-and-sport-anxiety-disorders.

Hatfield, Heather. "Sound Sleeping Key Part of Olympic Training," *Fox News*. February 15, 2006. http://www.foxnews.com/story/2006/02/15/sound-sleeping-key-part-olympic-training.html.

Klein, Christopher. "The First 4-Minute Mile, 60 Years Ago," *History*. May 6, 2014.https://www.history.com/news/the-first-4-minute-mile-60-years-ago.

Macmillan, Amanda. "The Mental Tricks Laurie Hernandez Uses to Summon Crazy Confidence," *Health*. August 11, 2016. http://www.health.com/mind-body/laurie-hernandez-confidence.

Malik, Zayn. "Zayn Malik: Why I Went Public With My Anxiety Issues," *Time*. October 31, 2016. http://time.com/4551320/zayn-malik-anxiety.

McAlindon, Harold R. "You Can if You Believe You Can—Reflections on Human Potential," *Success Unlimited*, 1978.

Melnick, Meredith. "The High Cost of Bad Sleep: $63 Billion Per Year," *Time*. September 1, 2011. http://healthland.time.com/2011/09/01/the-high-cost-of-bad-sleep-63-billion-per-year/.

Merriam-Webster Online Dictionary, s.v. "habit,"

"mindfulness," and "paradox." March 1, 2018, https://
www.merriam-webster.com.

Moore, Peter. "Two-Fifths Of Americans are Tired Most of
the Week," *YouGov.* June 2, 2015. https://today.you-
gov.com/news/2015/06/02/sleep-and-dreams/.

National Sleep Foundation, https://sleepfoundation.org.

Navarro, Manny. "Ray Allen's 'Crazy' Drills, Work Ethic
Remain Enduring Examples in Heat Locker Room," *Miami Herald.* November 1, 2016. http://www.miamiher-
ald.com/sports/nba/ miami-heat/article111840107.
html.

Nott, Laura. "Teens Are Feeling More Anxious Than Ever,"
Elements Behavior Health. July 2, 2013. https://www.
elementsbehavioralhealth.com/featured/teenagers-
are-feeling-more-anxious-than-ever/.

The Official Website of Geno Auriemma,
http://www.genoauriemma.com.

O'Kane, Josh. "1-on-1 with Drake: 'I'm going for the
$200-million play,'" *The Globe and Mail.* September
27, 2103. https://www.theglobeandmail.com/arts/
music/drake-i-may-as-well-be-in-charge-of-the-tour-
ism-board-in-canada/article14565583.

"Rats Dream About Their Tasks During Slow Wave Sleep,"
MIT News. May 18, 2002.   http://news.mit.
edu/2002/dreams.

Rehagen, Tony. "The Health Benefits of Gratitude,"
Success. October 5, 2017. https://www.success.com/
article/the-health-benefits-of-gratitude.

Schocker, Laura. "Your Body Does Incredible Things When
You Aren't Awake," *Huffington Post.* March 7, 2014.
https://www.huffingtonpost.com/2014/03/07/
your-body-does-incredible_n_4914577.html.

Stryker, Linda. "Meditation and the Mind." *Emeritus Voices
No. 10.* https://emerituscollege.asu.edu/sites/de-
fault/files/ecdw/EVoice10/meditation_and_mind.
html.

Television & Video References

"Bill Buckner: Behind the Bag." ESPN E: 60, October 25, 2011.

Franklin, James. "Why We Need Core Values," TEDxPSU. May 1, 2015. http://www.tedxpsu.com/videos/186.

Smith, Will. "Will Smith Shares His Secrets of Success and the Power of Visualization," YouTube interview compilation. October 22, 2014. https://www.youtube.com/watch?v=1lb8IzI4ApI.

 @COLLINHENDERSON

 COLLIN HENDERSON

WWW.THECOLLINHENDERSON.COM

PHOTO BY LACIE GORDON / LADI INFINITE PHOTOGRAPHY

254

ABOUT THE AUTHOR

Collin Henderson is a peak performance coach in the fields of athletics, business, and academics. He is an author, speaker, sales trainer, and mental conditioning instructor for a plethora of professional and amateur athletes, as well as business professionals.

He received his undergraduate degree in sports management, with an emphasis in business, and his master's in education from Washington State University. He was a standout starter in football and baseball—in which he was a captain, Pac-12 champion, and Academic All-American.

He has spent over eleven years as an award-winning, top-ranked territory manager and sales trainer with two Fortune 500 medical sales companies.

Collin, his wife Kendra, and their four children live in the suburbs of Seattle, Washington.

Visit thecollinhenderson.com and flowmentaltraining.com for more content, information, books, videos, and tools to improve your performance.

Made in the USA
Columbia, SC
26 July 2019